# BLISS

33 SIMPLE WAYS
TO AWAKEN
YOUR SPIRITUAL
SELF

## MICHAEL GODDART

Daybreak® Books
An Imprint of Rodale Press, Inc.
Emmaus, Pennsylvania

Daybreak is a registered trademark of Rodale Press, Inc.

Printed in the United States of America on acid-free ∞, recycled paper ♻

Jacket and Interior Designer: Mauna Eichner

**Library of Congress Cataloging-in-Publication Data**

Goddart, Michael.
    Bliss : 33 simple ways to awaken your spiritual self / Michael Goddart.
        p.        cm.
    ISBN 1–57954–079–1  hardcover
    1. Spiritual life.    I. Title
    BL624.G6    1999
    291.4'4—dc21                                              99–18116

**Distributed to the book trade by St. Martin's Press**

2    4    6    8    10    9    7    5    3    1    hardcover

Visit us on the Web at www.Rodalebooks.com or call us at (800) 848-4735

---

## OUR PURPOSE

*"We publish books that empower
people's minds and spirits."*

*for the true at heart*

*who are striving to*

*awaken further*

*always continue your journey*

*for each step will take you*

*closer to the bliss you are seeking*

# CONTENTS

## THREE

### Using Your Creative Imagination for Your Self

## FOUR

### Daily Disciplines for a Spiritual Foundation

## FIVE

### Practicing Spirituality in Your World

### SIX
## *Family and Friends*

### SEVEN
## *Inner Work*

### EIGHT
## *Spirituality without Judgment*

### NINE
*Forgiveness and Love*

# First This

You are a spiritual being. You possess within you a multitude of spiritual virtues and strengths in various stages of development.

To be spiritual is to exhibit these qualities of the pervading Spirit Force. Call it Spirit Force, Higher Power, God, Lord, or Supreme Being, this Higher Spirit to which we humans all have access has been called thousands of names throughout time. But this Power is unfathomable, inaccessible with our minds and thus unknowable with our minds, so any name we use is merely a convenient tag, a mode of reference. Use of *God* and *Lord* is not meant to convey that the Supreme Being is a masculine entity.

In a sense, all discussion is limiting, for the spiritual experience is direct and beyond language. But we must begin somewhere. Some of the things that this book suggests you do will lead you to a higher, direct experience of your spirituality and the Spirit within. The grace of the pervading Spirit Force to develop your spirituality is always available to you. Access to that Higher Power can be made through our consciousness. It's not that God is not out there—God or the Spirit Force does pervade all life—it's that God can be contacted within by purifying, concentrating, and raising our consciousness.

As we practice this natural process, as we play this song of love, we awaken our experience of the pervading unity of the Spirit Force, our Higher Power. *That experience of the unity of your Self and our Higher Power is bliss.* The capacity to experience that bliss is what makes us human. The experience of bliss is a spiritual one and can be received in a gamut of ways, from sitting in quiet meditation in remembrance of our Higher Power, to helping those in need with compassion, to feeling a state of equipoise while looking at a dandelion gone to seed. This capacity for bliss is available to all of us. Never for a moment judge yourself, thinking that you're not spiritual or that you're too dense or that you're simply not advanced enough. You can begin awakening to your spiritual Self right where you are. And you don't need to go on expensive retreats or suffer grueling austerities. It's a matter of consciousness. You can savor that bliss right in your own backyard.

Experiencing that bliss, that greater realization of God, can be achieved by developing the spiritual virtues. Take this journey, and together, page-by-page, we will experience and develop 33 essential spiritual virtues. Think of these 33 virtues as representing essential musical notes of the spiritual scale. The term virtues is meant to be all-encompassing, including what could also be called strengths, qualities, faculties, feelings, attitudes, activities, orientations, and practices. Virtue comes from the Latin *virtus*, meaning strength. Its archaic definition is the supernatural power or influence exerted by the Divine Being. Thus, when we are demonstrating virtues, we are expressing the divine within us. The Supreme Being is without attributes, yet paradoxically, it is the storehouse of all virtues and good qualities. The bottom line is that a person who is developing their spirituality will want to demonstrate these qualities in their everyday life.

That's what spirituality is. It's not taking off and cutting yourself off in a forest or desert or mountain hideaway, though these sojourns may certainly have their place. Spirituality is responsibly carrying out your duties to all those in your world. While developing a consciousness that is more and more of your Higher Power, your everyday behavior reflects the growing goodness, light, and love within you. The greater your realization of love—true, detached love—the greater your spirituality.

The spirituality offered here is universal. Its aim is not to convert you to any religion or group but to facilitate your growing relationship with your Higher Power, based on what Saints, those fully realized humans, have taught through the ages. If you follow a religion, doing these simple exercises and activities will make you a better Catholic, Jew, Baptist, Baha'i, Muslim, Methodist, or other follower.

What is offered here are simple things you can do to develop each of your 33 essential spiritual virtues. By performing these simple things, you begin to develop an inherent spiritual virtue or faculty. Our days are made up of mundane moments. One profound way of developing spirituality is to imbue these everyday moments with heightened consciousness and behavior that reflect a conscious connection to your Higher Power.

To this end, this guide is organized so that each virtue is discussed in a separate chapter, the title of which is a simple thing you can do to develop that virtue. The actual virtue may not be readily apparent and is usually not revealed until later in the section, and then it is given in bold type on the first two mentions. Part of the adventure of reading this book is the fun of guessing and discovering just which virtue is being explored. If you read and work with the guide from beginning to end, you'll find yourself taken through these 33 spiritual virtues in a nine-part natural progression: Opening to Spirituality, Your Relationship with Your Higher Power, Using Your Creative Imagination for Your Self, Daily Disciplines for a Spiritual Foundation, Practicing Spirituality in Your World, Family and Friends, Inner Work, Spirituality without Judgment, and Forgiveness and Love.

Focus on each chapter's heading as the simple way you can develop that spiritual virtue and awaken to your Higher Power. Within each chapter, specific exercises and activities are often explained. Don't feel constrained to do each of them as you read. Don't let yourself feel overwhelmed, but let yourself develop an inner knowing and readiness so that you act when the time is right for you. Some of the exercises may not appeal to you. Better things to do may come to you on your own, but look at this as an opportunity to really concentrate on learning about and developing your spirituality. You may wish to record your experiences with the exercises and activities in a journal. As you pursue your growth, please remember that these practices are useless unless performed with love. All practices, prayer, study, and worship are useless without love.

Also, reading a book to help yourself is good, but translating what you've begun to learn into sustained action is the true test of change. Thus, it's one thing to give up smoking at a health spa, yet quite another to not even be tempted at your favorite night spot with your friends puffing away. And certainly, it's easier to simplify your life by buying less stuff at garage sales, but all together different to give away all the possessions you don't really need so that you can focus on the spiritual stuff. Also be aware of the issue of commitment. It's one thing to buy a book on spirituality and flip through it during TV commercials, but another to reduce your TV time from 20 hours a week to 2, using that newly won time for your spiritual pursuit.

Always remember that you are closer and dearer to God than you can imagine. And as close as that Higher Power is to you, you can come ever more close as you raise your consciousness. With your next breath, you can begin opening more to spirituality. With this day, you can dedicate yourself anew to your growth. For now, put aside your preconceived ideas and judgments and know that you are a magnificent spiritual instrument, just ready to be tuned and cared for and played. Right now, you can begin a never-ending adventure that far exceeds your most glorious dreams. This song of love is yours for the playing. Your Higher Power is waiting to hear the exquisite music of your instrument. Let's start the playing.

# Opening to Spirituality

# Take a Walk

Take a walk and go somewhere where you'll find beautiful views. If you need a wheelchair, go out anyway; take a wheel. If you're confined to bed, just get close to an open window or, if possible, go outdoors. Take a journey in your mind.

Go alone and leave behind your radio or personal stereo, your beeper, your cellular phone, your dog, your mate. Go somewhere new or somewhere familiar that keeps drawing you back, because that feels good. As you walk, breathe in and breathe out. Be aware of breath filling you up, re-energizing your cells. Feel the fresh air on your face.

Continue to walk, and let your thoughts flow whichever way they will. If a problem is nagging you, work it out to the best of your ability. Then leave it behind. If it keeps clamoring for attention even though, for now, you've given it your best attention, tell it, "Be quiet." Keep insisting.

When you're ready, ask yourself, "What is the greatest gift I've been given?" Let the answer come to you. If you draw a blank, repeat the question. Keep walking.

Do you believe in God? Do you accept God? Even if you don't, why not try an experiment? Summon up your imagination—everyone has this ability—and imagine or visualize God; the Power that powers the universe; the Creator; the Source of Love, Forgiveness, and Mercy. If you wish to sit down and even close your eyes for this, do so. It isn't necessary, for you can feel God anytime, anyplace.

Now, feel God in all God's Glory giving you the greatest gift. What is it?

Keep walking, breathing in, breathing out. The Supreme Power, your Higher Power, is giving you the greatest gift. Just what is it?

Could it be your life? Your human life? What could be more basic, more important? Your human life is where it began for you, as far as you know. Take a deep breath and thank God. You can never thank God enough for your human life. It is precious beyond all reckoning.

With gratitude may come a desire to do something with your life. You may wish to make the best use of your life. Let yourself be filled with new air, new possibility. Let yourself be filled with *inspiration*.

*Inspiration* is an integral key to spirituality. When the going gets drab, when you forget where you are going, you need to inspire yourself, to fill yourself with new life. Life is Spirit. God is Life. When you take a walk, you are moving. You are leaving behind old places and going to new places. Even if you've seen the destination before, it is new because you have changed. You're in a new place. When you take a walk, you can make it a special, inspiring experience that is moving you more into spirituality, a spirituality that is rich with possibility. Remember, you are here for a purpose, a spiritual purpose.

# Wonder about the
# Four Immortal Questions

The four questions that humans have wrestled with through time are:

1. Who am I?

2. Where do I come from?

3. Where am I going?

4. What is God?

These questions are the beginning of the spiritual search, and the realization of their answers is the consummation of spirituality.

People who fear that they will be wasting their lives if they do not come to know their Selves and do not come closer to their Higher Power are lucky because they are open to spirituality. They are open to their unfolding.

❖    Exercise   ❖

Imagine a robot that is virtually human. It converses and works at the job that it's programmed for. It can do virtually anything, except it does not eat, eliminate, or have sex. It has no need to. It's powered by electricity. As long as it's powered up, it functions fine. When the electricity runs out, the robot can't do a thing. What do we humans have that works like electricity?

What if, when the parts of the robot begin to run down, the electricity is able to leave and enter a fresh new robot? There might be some similarities between the new and old robots, some impressions that carry over, but basically the new robot would not be able to remember its former existence.

❖    Exercise   ❖

After each of the following sentences or instructions, you may wish to pause and close your eyes and consider it fully. Take however long you wish.

Think of yourself and the place where you live and all the people who live in your town or city or surrounding area. Now, think of all the people and animals and plants that live in your county. Imagine different beings moving, eating, pursuing their lives. Think of all the living things — all the people and animals and plants and insects — that are living in your state. Now think of all the creatures of the land, sea, and air that live in your country. Imagine all the living creatures on our globe as it spins in space. Now, expand your imagination to encompass all the living things — even those you can't detect — of our galaxy. Finally, let your limitless imagination skim through all the living beings of the physical universe — even those living worlds many billion trillion light years away. Now, think of the force or energy that is *powering all that life*. Feel that life force, that creative power. Imagine the creative power that knows all. Are you a little awed?

❖ **Exercise** ❖

Do the following mentally, or if you wish, take a sheet of paper and draw a circle in the middle. In that circle, write, "Who am I?" Now, relax and let your mind go blank. Repeat the question and as soon as you have an answer, whether expressed in one or several words, write it a little distance from the main circle. Circle it and draw a connecting line to the main circle that holds your question. Continue to write down answers as fast as you can, drawing a circle around each one. The connecting lines will radiate out from the center or from answer to answer. It's all as you see it. You can work with this question by just wondering about it without paper, but when you brainstorm with great single-minded intensity, you will almost surely surprise yourself.

Repeat the exercise with the questions, "Where do I come from?" "Where am I going?" and "What is God?"

Look at the results. What you've written or thought is entirely, uniquely your own. It's your own expression. Different things may have opened up during this exercise. If they have, you have probably experienced some *awe*. *Awe* is just a word to denote a quality of spirituality that cannot be described. It's a noble emotion of wonder. It's having your mind blown while getting a glimmer of the unfathomableness of God. It's getting an understanding of who you are, individually and in the larger scheme of things. It's catching a ray of knowing the answer to where you come from and where you are going. Getting closer to the answers of these questions is receiving a peek of how exalted things are. And it's a promise of what can come.

If you believe that you feel awe, even if you're not really sure, just concentrate on it. Awe is an evolving feeling that becomes more profound and more full of wonder as your spirituality becomes focused and mature. The answers, as inarticulate as they may be, grow with the gathering of your spirituality. For now, feel awe if you have any deepening convictions about your spirituality. These convictions may be that you can come to know yourself, that there is an eternal power that is the All-Knowing Creative Power, that you've had an inkling that you can come to know God. Whatever convictions come now, love them, and when you ponder these questions, let yourself move with the awe.

# Open Your Heart and Turn to God

Whatever difficulties you're dealing with, it's tough. Whether it's illness, money problems, rough times in your marriage, worries over your child, being alone and lonely, struggling with an unfulfilling job or a difficult boss, the breakup of a relationship, making the grade in school, or living out your final years with respect and grace—your troubles weigh heavily on you.

Is there anyone who fully understands you, who knows and appreciates everything you're going through? There is. And though you could analyze how ultimately we've brought on our own troubles, we're here to turn to our Higher Power. You may have lost your faith and lost your way. That's understandable. How can you believe in something you can't see? But don't be misled by your lower mind. Your lower mind is that part of your mind that tends to generate thoughts and actions that take you away from God and from developing your inherent spiritual virtues.

Imagine a being that is all-understanding. This being has only one aim—your best interests. This being is all-loving. Think of a good, loving mother. While her child is playing just a few feet from her, she's content to let the child continue. But if the child hurts himself and starts to cry, the mother will rush to the child, pick up her darling, and comfort her little one. We are here to learn to turn to our Higher Power for just that comfort. And for every sincere step we take in that divine direction, our Higher Power will take at least 10.

Although it may seem to be a paradox, it is also true that your Higher Power is *inside* of you, closer than your breath and nearer than your thoughts. If you grew up thinking that God is a man or woman or power that is up *away* from you, in the sky or Heaven, looking down, hopefully benevolently, you've been, in a sense, misled. It's not a question of the physical—that the Power resides unimaginably far away from you or even that by making pilgrimages to special places or donning special clothes you can thereby get closer. It's a matter of consciousness. And our Higher Power has made it purely democratic in that each of us, each human being, has a personal temple in which to contact the Supreme Being. The approach to the entrance of that temple is where your attention is when you close your eyes. That is the start.

Please don't be apprehensive, thinking that it's an act of spiritual pride to concentrate your attention within to contact God. You're not praying to yourself, but focusing your attention, concentrating your consciousness, directly to contact that Higher Power of which you are a part and to which you are inescapably linked.

Though the love and prayers of others can make a tremendous difference, it's also not an act of personal folly to rely on yourself for strength and guidance. You're not relying on yourself, but availing yourself of that true support and contact that is your birthright. We aim to develop our own virtues because we each have our own channel to the Higher Power. As you clear your channel, you can begin to receive goodness and uplift from that limitless reservoir. Your all-knowing, all-loving God hasn't cast you to the bottom of a hierarchy, where you must rely on a person or power or system *outside* yourself for guidance and strength. Thank God, that isn't the case. You can begin to become more conscious of that connection right now, just as you are.

No matter how busy you are, set aside a time soon when you can be undisturbed and be with God. Make yourself comfortable in a quiet place and close your eyes. Now, just open your heart and turn to God and unburden yourself. Feel free to use words or just project feelings. The main thing is to have confidence that your Higher Power is right there, knowing everything, knowing you better than you know yourself, and pleased with you for turning within. Ask for your Higher Power's strength and love and grace to shoulder your burdens cheerfully and with a positive attitude. Opening your heart and seeking the sustenance of your Higher Power is ***prayer***.

There are no set requirements for ***prayer***. No special physical locations. No prescribed postures. No rituals. No rote sayings. The main thing about prayer is that it should come from the heart. Be honest, sincere, and earnest in giving vent to your innermost feelings. Also, be humble. Is it not the height of arrogance to tell or ask (that is, tell) that Power what we need? We are so sure of ourselves. Easily, we tell our Lord, "I need that hot new car, so-and-so to fall in love with me, a month in Maui, a million dollars, and, oh, yes, to get rid of this headache." Our so-called prayers can be an endless act of telling our Higher Power about what we need, for don't we *just know* what is for our good?

It is in God's power to do anything. Our Higher Power is also that Giver who can effortlessly create seeming miracles. But do we really know what is best for us and all the hows and whats of its immaculate delivery? If a child is sick with the stomach flu but crying for candy, does a good mother give her little one that candy or does she give the child medicine to heal the illness? We really don't know what is best for our spiritual benefit. What we want and what is best for us may be quite different. But to turn within for help with problems and burdens, all the time feeling, "Thy good Will be done," is giving our problems to God and asking for God. That is true prayer. That is opening yourself to transformation.

# TWO

# Your Relationship with Your Higher Power

# Decide to Develop
# Your Potential for God

Considering that you're reading this book and you have accepted that there may be things you can do to develop your spirituality, then to some extent you've accepted the fact that you're a spiritual being. Hopefully, as you work and play with these suggestions, you'll open more than before to the higher knowing, clearer intuition, selfless love, and reasonless bliss that are available to you.

It is difficult to work toward realizing the transforming spiritual virtues and attributes, because, by definition, spiritual experience is subtle, not intellectual, not sensual, and easily missed. It's much easier to pursue the obvious satisfactions of a good meal, a funny situation comedy, an exciting game, or whatever gives you pleasure. Consider what it would have been like if you had spent your entire high school career cutting class, getting high, and goofing off. Having failed to graduate, you would have found most paths barred. Entire worlds would be closed to you and you'd have no idea of what you were missing! But life is a school, and just by showing up, paying attention, and doing your schoolwork, you can reap rewards so sweet, so great, so full of wonder, that now you can barely begin to imagine them.

Certainly, you have your own array of desires that seek satisfaction. To some extent, spiritual desires may be part of that. If you accept that you are a spiritual being, why not accept that your imagination can barely begin to envision what you may attain? Why not accept that you can attain an existence of love, joy, peace, and knowing that you can, indeed, advance in the realization of God?

Becoming aware of the possibility is a first step. Wishing it to happen is another step. But this will fall away as an idle fancy unless you form the *desire* and *decide to develop your potential for God*. And you won't ever begin to develop your spiritual potential until you form the *intention* to advance your desire for God. *Desire* and *intention* for God are the fundamental spiritual virtues. When energized and focused, they combine to form a powerful will. That will is necessary for overcoming the mind's dominating lower tendencies so that you actually advance on your upward path.

If spirituality is the growing realization of our divinity, then desire is the fuel that will get us there. After all, it was desire for things of the world that first pulled us away from God.

Understand desire, and you understand happiness and unhappiness. If desire is the fuel, intention is the engine. Intention is the strength of purpose and will that powers you up past the steep inclines and keeps you chugging along over the bogs. Without intention to utilize your desire, the desire will pool in your mind, dormant like the gas in the tank of a car that sits idle in a garage. And unless you periodically fuel your intention with desire, you'll sputter to a stop despite the best intentions.

The unabating desire for things of this world—money, sex, fame, name, people, beauty, bodies—with all their particular insistent requirements, keeps us revved up, falsely advertises the destination "Happiness," and keeps us cruising down those roads. But when and if we ever arrive, we're never there. At least not for long.

Why not take this opportunity to begin to explore your option for *lasting* happiness? This destination is hard to realize; it's ever so subtly placed on a far higher plane. But this plane is available to you, and once you get a taste, you'll want more and more. So, why not try the high road? You can't begin to dream of the new places to which renewing your relationship with your Higher Power will take you.

## ❖ Resolution ❖

Make a commitment to yourself to energize your desire and intention for God. If you don't like the name God, use another. Spirit. Ram. Allah. Lord. Goddess. Higher Power. How about Love? Beloved? Or no name? The important thing is to recognize that you have unlimited ability and power within yourself to develop your spirituality. Now, concentrating your will, make the resolution within yourself.

Don't just make the resolution and leave it at that. Link it now to something that you feel will advance you on your path of growing awareness. Perhaps it's using a journal to help take you through all these suggestions. Perhaps the first action will be to do something that's been speaking to you louder and louder, like curbing your anger and being kind. Once you make your resolution and remake it and make it again so that it is firmly rooted in your consciousness, the next step will present itself. Perhaps your next step is exploring just what your relationship with your Higher Power is.

Once you have energized the intention of realizing God, every effort you make and every step you take, even if it's something as innocent as taking a walk, is valuable toward realizing your true objective. That's because you are advancing on the path that is leading you to your true objective. Perhaps your next step is finding out what the Saints have written about the experience of God, or simply wondering what could possibly lie ahead if you embark on this path of eternal adventure. Once you accept that you have unlimited potential for God, the possibility of amazing things opens up.

# Spend Two Minutes a Day with Your Higher Power

As you pray and spend more time contacting your Higher Power, the feeling and conviction may grow within you that much, much more is possible spiritually than you ever allowed. Regardless of who you are and what you've done, an Ocean of Comfort, Love, and Truth is available to you. You have the power within you to realize God.

Just spending two minutes a day contacting your Higher Power can be the start of a truly new life, an adventure filled with wonder and love, the love you can keep, always. Realize, please, that you've been given the greatest gift anyone can receive: a human life. It is difficult to really appreciate and understand just how precious, just how great it is that you are living now as a human.

With problems stacking up, crowding in on you, it's easy to lose sight of that sublime opportunity. Everything demands its own time in your life. Every life is fraught with its own difficulties. We struggle and struggle with our lives, trying to make them right, yet before we're ready and willing, they're over. And as we struggle, we expend time. As we work, fulfill our family duties, take care of our physical needs, grains of sand are running through our own egg timers. Those grains are numbered. Eventually, they run out.

*Time is your most precious commodity.* The easiest thing to put off is your spirituality, yet that is what is most important. It's never too late to reclaim your lost inheritance.

## ❖ Exercise ❖

Spend two minutes a day with your Higher Power. Please follow these steps.

1. Choose a time when you know you can be quiet and undisturbed. That time should be a time that you can pretty much rely on to be yours alone each day: after you get up in the morning; at night, while your partner is reading in

bed; when you get home from work; at lunchtime, before you return to work; or, if there simply isn't a time at home or work that you can count on, perhaps you can schedule two minutes during your morning commute.

2. Make yourself comfortable. Take a deep breath. Close your eyes.

3. Now, how do you give your two minutes to God? Talk to God, pray to God, or be silent. Open your heart. Just be with God. If you like to call your Higher Power by a particular name, you can repeat that name. Don't keep checking the clock. Let yourself know when the two minutes are up. Then open your eyes. That's it.

What you need to remember is, practice makes perfect. Just starting to sit regularly and punctually for two minutes a day in contact with your Higher Power could ultimately transform you into a Saint. Spirituality is attained by *practice*. *Practice* is the essential virtue for making spiritual progress. When you practice, you are giving time, your most precious commodity. When you are giving time, engaging in spiritual practice with humility and sincerity, you can invoke grace and become more receptive to God.

Spirituality is practice. While reading to attain spiritual theories has its place, particularly when you are seeking, if you just read and write about spirituality, it will remain dormant. Spirituality mus[t] awakened, developed, and lived. That is why practice is the true beginning of spirituality and the means to its realization.

In practicing this exercise, the best thing is to choose a particular time and stick to it. The mornings, first thing after you get up, may be the best time. Why not make your spirituality your first priority and start the day with it? Once you've been able to give 2 minutes regularly, you may choose to increase your time to 5 minutes a day. This may be after a month or a year. The main thing is to first solidify your progress and then increase it. At your own speed, you may eventually increase your time giving to 10 minutes, 20 minutes, even two hours.

As with all endeavors in life, but particularly with spirituality, the secret of success is practice, practice, practice, practice, practice.

# When You Brush Your Teeth, Come to Attention and Salute

Most people brush their teeth twice a day, day in, day out. The minutes accumulate into hours, the hours into days, and typically, in a lifetime, a person spends the equivalent of 106 days brushing their teeth. When you brush your teeth, what do you think about? You probably have no idea. During this one mundane activity, a significant chunk of your life, your time is ruled by random thoughts.

If time is our most precious commodity, then *attention* is our most precious resource. The ability to consciously direct *attention* is a prime human attribute and power. So, as we spend our lives brushing our teeth, flossing our teeth, shaving, washing, grooming, dressing, walking to the car or transit stop, driving, waiting for lights to change, elevators to come, and commercials to end, where is our attention? The prime resource of attention is left undeveloped. Our minds are left to play over and over things like advertising that's washed our brains or upsets that are not resolved. The tendency is to not use the vital resource of attention. Meanwhile, the grains of time are passing inexorably through our individual egg timers. Yet these otherwise wasted moments can be directed toward our Higher Power, toward building spiritual wealth. With practice, anyone can experience a lifting of consciousness and bliss.

Our days are made up of mundane moments. One profound way of developing spirituality is to imbue these everyday moments with heightened consciousness.

### ❖ Exercise ❖

When you brush your teeth, come to attention and salute the Higher Power within you. To *salute* is to greet with a gesture showing recognition, respect, and honor. When you put your toothbrush to your mouth, that is the outer gesture, but as you do it, also think that you're performing an inner gesture: a bow, and a kiss of love, awe, and affection for the Higher Power within you.

*Come to attention* is a catch phrase that means different things according to your practice. If you have a particular technique of repetition or meditation, you may use that. If not, try this.

### ❖ Exercise ❖

First, just be aware that you can be aware. Next, visualize that you're watching a film projected onto a screen. The film is a record of your random automatic thinking, the common noise, the chatter—the series of unfocused thoughts and images over which you generally have no control. Now, stop the film on one frame. Notice the light shining through the frame, projecting it as a picture. *That light* is a focused beam from your consciousness. Now, using your consciousness, turn the light away from the frozen frame of your random thoughts and shine it around inside itself, in your forehead, illuminating your internal sense of awareness and being. Come to attention, be aware of your awareness being aware, and be in contact with God. Remember, your Higher Power is inside of you, closer than your breath and nearer than your thoughts. Sense the stillness behind your thoughts. Without a mind that is quiet and attentive, you'll miss that stillness as you let it chatter away.

As we develop attention, we're also developing the qualities of alertness and present mindfulness. With alertness, we are readier to catch our awareness as it goes off on a tangent. Thus, we are more fully conscious, more aware. With present mindfulness, we're existing more fully in the present. We're not dwelling in the past nor are we obsessing over the future. When we allow consciousness to get entangled in the past or future, we're trafficking in the illusion of time. Since God is beyond time, which is an illusion fed by our minds, we must seek God in the eternal now. As our attention grows less scattered and more concentrated in the present, which is the point of power, we are better able to pierce the great subtleties of Spirit. Concentrated attention, alertness, and present mindfulness are necessary to pursue the spiritual journey. Without developing these faculties, we continue to be led astray by our minds.

This is a lifelong journey to imbue your everyday life with spirituality. Everything you do, every thought you think, is an opportunity to make progress. Ultimately, spirituality will spread through your life like a brilliant dye coloring a plain cloth. Thus, start with something perfectly mundane. While brushing your teeth, eyes open or closed, come to attention, and acknowledge that Spirit behind your thoughts. Salute the God within you, and as your attention focuses, watch your relationship grow.

# Today, Be a Goodwill Ambassador

*I*f God is within you, is God perhaps in others? God doesn't play favorites. Your Higher Power is present in everyone, regardless of creed, color, caste, condition, or conduct. We are all of the same strain. The differences and divisions that we recognize are false. They're barriers that we've let our lower minds erect. Thus, we keep thinking that we're separate from our fellow humans, and so we strive for self-gratification.

The Supreme Power, a spiritual force, can't exist in all its unalloyed glory and power in this physical world, yet that Power is present in all living things in varying degrees of consciousness. As humans, we have the inherent capacity to fully realize our spirituality.

If we're interested in developing our spirituality, in pleasing the Supreme Being, then we can endeavor to behave in ways that are spiritual and pleasing to the Lord. By reading this book and others on spirituality, you should be able to develop a clear idea of what constitutes spirituality. By acting on that, exerting the will of your higher mind, you will have the power to develop along more spiritual lines. By striving to think and act from your center of truth and love, you are developing spiritually in a way that can impact others positively.

Thus, if you accept the power of God within you, *you have the power to act as God's agent*. Therefore, why not act as if you're God's goodwill ambassador? You certainly have the power to do so. Why not try it? Just for today.

### ❖ Activity ❖

Today, act as though you're God's goodwill ambassador. Start by greeting from your heart the next person you see, silently acknowledging the spark of divinity within that person. Don't unnecessarily intrude, but if you run across someone you know or if it's appropriate with someone you don't know, say a simple "Hello." As you greet the person, acknowledge that you're saluting the Higher Power within that person. Continue to greet those whom you meet appropriately, silently conveying the acknowledgment of the spark of divinity you share.

When you're acting as a goodwill ambassador, you are wishing goodness for all people you meet. You are rising above differences and the false boundaries of race, station, and belief to honor and salute your inter-connectedness as human beings. You're also wishing that good will—God's good will—be done. When you meet someone, the waves of good will that you send include love. Your loving wishes are reaching those whom you meet, washing over them, uplifting them, and in effect, raising their consciousness. You're practicing the important virtue of *agenting*. We all have the capacity to act as humble agents of God. *Agenting* is a great gift and opportunity and spiritual attribute.

Of course, care must be taken to be a *humble* agent. Be wary of traps. For instance, don't let your mind persuade you that by converting people to your beliefs or your religion, you're doing good. Religious warriors who put infidels to death may ardently believe that they are God's agents gaining eternal paradise. But if you wish to be a spiritual warrior, wage a war against your own lower tendencies and be an example to others by endeavoring to act as a loving agent of God. Agenting is a simple act offered purely out of humility and recognizing the divinity of those you meet and wishing them goodness, love, and grace. When performed in humility, agenting extends to your fellow beings your relationship with your Higher Power, in such a way that they're uplifted and empowered and brought subtly into an enhanced relationship with their Higher Power. By acting simply as a goodwill ambassador, you are revering that glorious Higher Power within us all.

# THREE

# Using Your Creative Imagination for Your Self

# Put On Your Own Class Reunion

*I*t's one thing to acknowledge the spark of divinity within friends and strangers yet quite another to be a true goodwill ambassador to those who have made you feel bad and mad and less than you are. Those who were with you in school affected you when you were vulnerable. Upon graduation, you may have wished to never see some classmates again. Meanwhile, you may have cared desperately what others would think about you if you were to meet them again. Guess what? You're in luck. You can see those schoolmates again.

Ah, class reunions, those affairs that we look forward to yet attend with great fear and loathing as well as anticipation. Why are they so terrible? So dreaded? So important? In high school, we stood on the threshold of adulthood, ready to win the world. At reunions, we go back, ready to submit to judgments by old pals and enemies who now look different. (Hopefully, they're different in a kinder, gentler way. And more hopefully, we've aged in a kinder, gentler way.) We return to our peers, who will discover how we've aged and what we've amounted to. Often, it's a surprise — a reversal of the roles we played in high school. The paradigm for men is the class geek who comes back a self-assured millionaire and the class football hero who slinks back bald, hoping that no one knows he pumps gas for a living.

Why are class reunions so dreaded? Many of us care desperately about what people will think of us and how they'll judge us. And we adopt those judgments, whether real or perceived, as our own. In high school, most of us did much to be accepted. Alternatively, some of us worked hard to not be accepted by the "in" crowd and succeeded well, indeed.

Even if we never attend a class reunion, many of us have enacted them in our heads. Many of us avoid ours because we're too embarrassed about what we've not become. Have you ever considered having a hair transplant or a face-lift? Have you ever bought an expensive luxury car or piece of jewelry? If you were going to your 20th high school reunion, would you consider doing one of these things or making some other change? Here's something that's less painful, cheaper, and ultimately more satisfying.

❖    **Exercise**    ❖

Read through this exercise twice, then close your eyes and imagine the following. Your high school class is having a reunion this very evening. See yourself getting ready for the big night, shaving or putting on makeup, fixing your hair, getting dressed, looking in the mirror, taking stock. How do you feel about yourself?

See yourself driving to your reunion and telling yourself that none of this really matters, yet a certain anticipation makes you speed up then slow down. See yourself all dressed up, walking into a strange hotel lobby. What are you thinking? How do you feel about yourself? See yourself nearing a group of people. How do you feel about meeting those people who knew you as a teenager?

See people whom you can almost but not quite place coming up to you to read your name tag while you glance at theirs. Visualize your old friends and foes. How do your old friends react? Your former enemies and nemeses? Who is it that you're most anxious about meeting? Visualize them coming up to you. Now, see yourself talking to them. Imagine that they are forming opinions or judgments about you. See those judgments coming out of their heads, taking shape like sticky ectoplasm, coming at you, glomming on, but then sliding off, leaving you unscathed. Surrounding you is your very own invisible protective shield, the conviction that you are fine just the way that you are. Say, "I accept and love myself just as I am and as I am not." Repeat this until you are ready to move on.

## ❖ Continuing Exercise ❖

Now, see the people whom you remember and care most about coming up to you and seeing you. Guess what? Your invisible shield has another magical property; it enables people to see, perfectly, you and everything you've done in your life. It's as if they can see a speeded-up movie of everything you've done. Now, those people are standing before you, and your whole life is flashing before them. Let them see the things that most embarrass or shame you.

The scenes of your life end. See and hear the people, one by one, saying to you, "_____ (your name), I accept you and love you just as you are." See the people at your reunion coming up to you and saying, "_____ (your name), I accept you and love you just as you are."

After the last person has come up to you, take stock of how you feel. When you're ready, open your eyes.

## ❖ Activity ❖

If you're moved to, write about how you're feeling now. On a sheet of paper, write the words "my self" and draw a circle around them. Then, let yourself go, and write the words and phrases that just come to you, drawing circles around them and drawing lines to connect the circles. Don't censor anything. Whatever words or phrases come to you, put them down on paper. Keep building your cluster of circles, and this time, if you feel an urge, *when you feel moved to*, on another side of paper, write a paragraph or vignette about "my self." When you're finished, congratulate yourself for writing a lovely piece, and reread it. What does it say or intimate about acceptance?

A successful class reunion is when people come together in the spirit of acceptance rather than judgment. It won't work for you if you attend while feeling any sense of shame or blame or a lack of *self-acceptance*. *Self-acceptance* is the essential spiritual virtue for allowing the spiritual work to proceed naturally. Lack of self-acceptance can signal a major obstacle. It can impede your spiritual development by not allowing your Higher Power to work in you and through you. To understand why, let's further explore what nonacceptance is.

First, when you are in any way not accepting of yourself, you're simply denying the reality of the situation. You are resisting what is so. Let's assume that you have chronic fatigue syndrome, but you deny it and push yourself so much that you make yourself worse. Perhaps, in getting ready for your reunion, you run around shopping for the perfect new outfit, going to the beauty salon, getting in extra sessions in the tanning booth, pumping iron to show off your biceps, and taking only diet drinks. Well, then, the evening of the reunion, you could very well end up in a state of total exhaustion and be forced to stay home. If, in spite of not feeling up to it, you push yourself to attend, that could really worsen your chronic fatigue syndrome.

On the other hand, if you focus on self-acceptance when you begin to get apprehensive about how you'll look at the reunion, accepting the reality that you have chronic fatigue syndrome and need to really take care of yourself, you may do those things that are truly nurturing and that support your energy. When it's time to get ready for your evening of close encounters, you might not look as tanned and sleek as you'd like, but you'll have plenty of energy to attend your reunion, and you'll be more likely to greet your former classmates with an inner glow.

Second, when you're lacking self-acceptance, you can also deny the present, dwelling in your mock-up of another time that right now does not exist. Perhaps in high school you were a cheerleader with a perfect figure, but now, after having a couple kids and not watching what you eat . . . well, let's just say that more than your personality is expansive. Now, if you attempt to squeeze into your old uniform because your consciousness is so enmeshed in the past that you believe you still have a perfect figure and can't accept that now it is simply re-sized, you could end up bursting that uniform. Or, if you are able to squeeze in, you could look mighty ridiculous. Thus, being self-accepting means being in the present in addition to accepting reality. When you're dwelling in this place, you are empowered to proceed forward, progressing with all your work.

A third element of nonacceptance of self is finding fault. Finding fault is deciding what you don't like, what is "wrong." It's forming an opinion based on a view of things that is often narrow, restricted, or lacking in information and understanding. When you find fault with yourself, you pass judgment on yourself. Spirituality is acting from a place of truth, of love, while not judging.

Do some quiet reflection to determine in which part of your high school career you were judged most harshly. Perhaps the coach or team leader always yelled at you and was never happy with your performance. To what extent did you take in this negativity? Perhaps in softball you were always put in right field. It was common knowledge that you couldn't catch; you were a spaz. On the rare occasion that a fly ball came your way and another player couldn't get over to take away your chance, you usually missed the catch. After your failed attempt, the jeers and shrugs of disgust pierced you to the quick. You became convinced that you really were a screwup, a lousy ballplayer. Self-loathing and rejection grew in your heart, and soon you found ways of cutting phys ed.

But what if, the next year, a kindly teacher happened to suggest that you have an eye exam and you discovered that you were near-sighted? Eventually, you may have discovered that you were actually quite coordinated and not at all a spaz. But even if you weren't nearsighted, your below-average performance was probably reinforced by and partly caused by *your believing and embracing* the negative judgments of peers, teachers, and parents. Would you embrace a person who is a liar, thief, and serial killer? No, but that's what you do when you embrace others' negative judgments about yourself. You're accepting lies about yourself; you're giving others the power to steal your freedom; and you're letting those closest to you kill your life. Think about it.

To go forward, to successfully meet your own life challenges, and to grow spiritually, you need all the self-acceptance, love, and self-approval that you can give yourself. When you find fault with yourself, you are actually finding fault with the manifestation of the Will of the Higher Power. You're putting your own limited knowledge, your view of only a small part of the picture, and your *judgment* ahead of the Universal Power's knowledge.

We have limited self-knowledge and don't fully comprehend the challenges and liabilities with which we come into the world.

Also, do we fully recall and understand just what happened to us during our childhoods and how that affected us? Do we have such evolved knowing and consciousness that we can see and understand why things are happening to us and how things are happening for our higher good and our spiritual growth?

You can pass judgment that not succeeding the way that *you want* is a terrible thing. But that immediate lack of success may actually be the best thing right now for your spiritual growth. Your challenge is to discern what steps are appropriate for you now without sinking into a funk. Self-acceptance is very different from being passive. For instance, you can fully accept the fact that you haven't made manager or partner yet and feel *good* about yourself while *continuing your efforts* to progress at work and discerning what aspects of your character you may work on improving.

Self-acceptance is recognizing how things truly are, while at the same time working on your goals. To be grounded in the present, to operate from that point of power, you need to accept yourself fully.

When you don't accept yourself fully, you indulge negative ego. Egotism is the force that separates us from our Higher Power. Usually, we think of egotism as being all puffed up with pride: "I'm the hottest partner that this firm has ever had." Or, "I have the most flawless face and body that a woman can have." But egotism can just as easily be negative self-obsession: "How did I ever get my law degree? Now, I wouldn't even be able to pass traffic school." Or, "I look like I woke up in a trash compactor."

Rather than being obsessed with yourself in an inflated or deflated way, you wish to develop self-acceptance that is based on clear-eyed, even-handed self-knowledge. You will have egotism until you become quite advanced spiritually, and as you progress, you can strive to develop a healthy, balanced ego. Part of treading the spiritual path is discovering and coming to know just who you are. This knowledge is crucial as you work with your ego to wean it from unfulfilling patterns and downward tendencies. This self-knowledge facilitates practicing the spiritual virtues.

As a healthy, knowing parent, once you truly know your children, you can successfully guide them through their tantrums and facilitate their learning. Likewise, learning about yourself leads to self-acceptance and effective working with yourself so that you begin to attain spiritual maturity.

Even though you begin to grow in spiritual maturity, you may still *unconsciously* carry a lack of self-acceptance with you into all kinds of circumstances. Whenever you find yourself feeling uncomfortable or afraid or leery of a situation, repeat the affirmation "I am perfect as I am and as I am not."

In an earlier exercise, you visualized your high school peers while repeating an affirmation. An affirmation is a saying or statement that can be repeated mentally, verbally, or in writing. Affirmations can be positive or negative, formal or automatic. Most of us are adept at automatically repeating negative affirmations throughout the day. Recall what you *kept thinking* during the reunion exercise or an actual reunion as you entered the lobby. Was it, "God, I look like a cow," "This suit looks cheap," or "I bet I've aged more than anyone here"? If you were thinking anything like that, you were repeating negative affirmations. Rather than engage in this negative brainwashing, why not conduct your own positive brainwashing, enhancing the possibility for your spiritual virtues to grow?

## ❖ Affirmation ❖

First, visualize yourself as a teenager or at whatever stage at which you've felt most uncomfortable. See, feel, and sense yourself at that age. Be yourself at that time and repeat, "I am perfect as I am and as I am not." Notice what feelings, images, thoughts, and judgments this brings up. Practice being a mature, patient teacher and show your teenager just why you are perfect as you are and as you are not.

Whenever you notice yourself judging yourself or giving power to others' judgments, repeat this exercise. By doing so, you're uprooting your weeds of negative ego and nurturing your beautiful spirit to grow. Always remember that, most of the time, what you imagine or perceive to be nonacceptance is actually your projection, your imagining. But others' opinions, actual or imagined, can have no effect on you unless you give them power and allow them to. Even if someone doesn't accept you, it's your taking in their lack of acceptance that gives power — negative power — to that judgment. And that erodes your virtue of self-acceptance.

Through this exercise, hopefully, you've achieved a recognition of your unique self and moved closer to reunion with your self. This is a first step of self-realization: going back to who you really are. All judgments are stripped away. This empowers you to develop self-acceptance, to go forward and rise above petty, constricting judgments so that your soul begins to be prepared for that higher reunion with your Higher Power.

# Start Your Own Peanut Gallery

The Peanut Gallery was a regular feature of the *Howdy Doody* show, hosted by Buffalo Bob Smith, which ran on television from 1947 to 1960. The Peanut Gallery was the audience of children. It was the most special treat to be a part of the Peanut Gallery, watching and, in some cases, getting to participate in the action.

Before you go through the magical steps of forming your own peanut gallery, revisit what you were like as a child to get an idea of what your experience may have been.

## ❖ Activity ❖

Gather all the photo albums, videos, and movies of you from the age of 18, going back all the way to when you were born. Starting with the most recent albums and videos, look at yourself and really get a sense of yourself as a child. When did you look most happy? When did you look pained? What kinds of connections did you seem to have with your parents and those around you?

In addition to freeing yourself of negative judgments so that you can inculcate self-acceptance, it's also possible to use your creative imagination to free yourself of entangled energies that may not be your own. These alien energies, in effect, are cords tying you to other people, sapping you of your independent strength. How can you tread a path if you're always being pulled back? How can you awaken to your true higher Self if you're carrying within you the emotional patterns and thought forms of others and if you've internalized others' judgments, which are sourced in their trials and failures and are not your reality?

Just because you can't physically see all this gunk, doesn't mean it's not real. If, every time you want to do a certain action, a self-defeating argument takes over and these inner voices are draining you of your independent power, how real is that? How free are you? If you try to take a step in the direction from which your higher Self hears a call and, with that step, your leg is held back by invisible cords and your heart is troubled and your mind confused, how free are you? If you can't even find your direction, because you're so all-over-the-place, wouldn't you like to move closer to your true, free Self? Working through these issues can be many years' work, but try this exercise.

## ❖ Exercise ❖

In bed one night when you're feeling restless or troubled or alone, let your imagination find your inner wonder child. Your inner child is the child that you are still carrying with you in spirit. Even though years have passed, part of you is still the child that you once were. You may think that child is gone, but that child is still with you, with its own needs and magical capabilities. Actually, you have an inner child or teenager for each year before you became an adult. Your inner wonder child is that child who possessed and possesses the greatest promise, purity, independence, true sense of self, and wonder.

Call within for your wonder child to come to you. When you feel, or in your mind's eye see, a presence, ask your inner child how old he or she is. Look at your wonder child, full of aliveness and promise. Hug your child. Now, tell your wonder child that you're going to go on a journey. Take the child's hand and ask to be taken to your mother. Let your mother be whatever age and live in whatever home that you wish to see in your vivid imagination. If she's deceased, let your wonder child lead you to a time when she was alive. If you didn't know your mother, visit the person who most embodied that role.

Now, see what cords, like umbilical cords, are connecting you and your wonder child to your mother. You may have many, but this special inner child has one or none. The cords will generally be connecting to your energy centers: your navel, representing power; your genitals, for sexuality and creativity; your tailbone and adrenals, for survival; your heart, for love; your throat, for communication and identity; and your forehead, for your conscious mind and belief systems.

See the cords connecting you both to her. See what they represent and how they engender your dependence, sapping you of your own innate vitality. Now, tell her that this won't hurt her or you a bit, and tell her that you love her *and* that you are removing all the cords. With your wonder child, remove them first from her and then from yourselves, using whatever means feels right. Remove them with ease or pull on them till they pop off or simply rip them out. How do they feel? How do they smell? What do they look like? Do they have lives of their own?

Toss them in a heap on the ground and use your creative imagination to find the appropriate, effective means for their elimination.

For instance, focusing your attention and intention, see them wither and shrivel up and turn to dust under the hot noon sun. Or, in your mind's eye, take out a ray gun and vaporize them. Or, dig a six-foot-deep hole and bury them. Or, take a gallon of gasoline, saturate the cords with the gasoline, step back, light a match, and toss it on the heap. Watch the fire consume it until nothing remains.

Tell your mother that you still love her and that now you are a completely separate, integrated person. Ask her if she's happier now that she's gained more independence. If it feels right, hug her and kiss her. Tell her that you have your own power sourced in yourself, independent of what she thinks, says, does, or wants. Tell her that you're leaving with your child and from now on you are living your own life, taking care of yourself. Embrace your child and say, "I am now your good parent, your all-knowing parent who knows and needs your desires."

Your mother is the person with whom you have primal bonds. Most likely, it will be necessary to repeat this exercise with the images of your father, your partner, and any grandparents, siblings, lovers, mentors, or friends with whom you don't feel complete freedom and support in being your true self. With the cords tying you to your primary influences gone, you are now empowered to practice *autonomy*. *Autonomy* is a crucial spiritual strength that is necessary for you to evolve into your higher Self. Autonomy not only is freedom from external influences but also is the power to govern yourself independently and to follow your own true path.

A person who is autonomous is operating from their spiritual center. They are free of negative influences, and when and if they do get corded back into a relationship, they utilize their power to re-free themself and re-establish themself in their spiritual center.

An autonomous person self-directs their life. They are where they are now, and their power is always growing and being utilized to express their highest Self and to manifest their higher purpose. An autonomous person *celebrates* their interconnectedness with others, and because they have realized their healthy separation from family, they can achieve that healthy balance between independence and interconnectedness.

Realizing your autonomy is removing limits and self-defeating patterns. It's freeing yourself to go where no one else but you can go. It's claiming your very own mountain and setting out for the summit with your backpack brimming with provisions and virtues and strengths. But as you climb toward the summit, it can get cold and lonely.

At those times, those old attachments and cordings with parents and others can look like a safety rope. Even as you develop your relationship with your Higher Power so that your spiritual Self comes to the fore, you can convince yourself, even quite unconsciously, that to continue the ascent you need to continue those old relationship patterns. You remember them as being so familiar, so comforting. Unfortunately, you forget that those cords were, in fact, twisted around your chest and neck, choking you. It's tempting to reach for those ropes, for in the past you may have even tightened those attachments or cordings with parents and others because you felt so alone and powerless. But that won't help. You've been climbing. You need a rarer air.

Take heart, you are not alone. You do have your Higher Power, and soon, equally autonomous friends will come into your life to further you on your journey. Still, when you are bereft and waiting on a deserted plateau for someone, for anything, you are never alone. To prove it, try this exercise.

### ❖ Exercise ❖

Using your creative imagination, call on your wonder child to come before you. It's likely that this child looks more alive than ever. Now, in any order you choose, call on all your inner children from birth to age 18 to visit you. Since you have destroyed the cords that bound them, they are tremendously vital and embody their best, most powerful qualities. What are they like, this family of selves? Are you surprised by any of your children? Sometimes, a child will embody a particular quality. Ask whether you have a child who is your adventure child, discovery child, bravery child, study child, magic child, healing child, prince or princess child, intuition child, or any other. Let them come before you and interact with you.

Now, tell them that you're starting a peanut gallery and you want them all, even your most rebellious teenagers, to be part of it. Their job will be to enjoy the show that is your life and, when you need special assistance, to come on stage and render that assistance. They'll also be able to call out from their gallery and make noises when they need to be heard and when they need your attention. When you've lost your way and you're confused and feeling weak, you can call on them to help you through. Your peanut gallery is with you to guide you, to let you have fun, and to let you imbibe those qualities that further your mastery of autonomy.

Let your children know, to their delight, that you are on the road *home* to your own Oz-like kingdom where you will join with the all-benevolent, self-governing monarch. Along the way, you may commit actions that you regret. You may say terrible things that you wish you could take back, but you are coming into your own. As you continue to work and play with the virtues, you are freeing yourself of negative influences and returning to your spiritual Self. You are learning how to negotiate your own path, on your own, with a sense of adventure, discovery, bravery, study, magic, healing, intuition, autonomy, wonder, and love.

# Take a Vacation

Taking a vacation can be a wonderfully spiritual thing to give yourself. It offers the opportunity for rest, renewal, and reawakening to just who you really are. Once the competing demands and pressures from your everyday world begin to fall away, wonderful, authentic feelings come through. You may decide to make changes in your life when you return, to simply "be" in a different mode, or to stress certain new priorities.

## ❖ Activity ❖

Go on vacation. It can be one day, overnight, or several weeks. Near or very far. When you take off, make a pact with yourself that you simply won't think about things in your everyday world unless you do it at a designated time. For instance, there may be an issue that's weighing on you—a problem with a child or at work. Make a pact that you won't think about it until a certain time, say, the evening of the fourth day of your trip.

Meanwhile, do the things that appeal strongly to you, those things that are restful and fun. Don't make yourself do things out of a sense of duty. Don't think, "This is the only time I'll have to read this hot new management book. I better read it." Or, "I bought all this expensive scuba diving gear; I'm going to use it every day." Just listen to your body. Do what it wants. It gets flogged enough as it is.

If you can take this vacation alone, that's good. Try not to take it with a significant other unless you are mutually aligned and that person truly supports you in your spiritual growth. During the vacation, try the following exercise several times.

### ❖ Exercise ❖

Re-read these directions carefully until you really understand what they're getting at. Try this exercise while taking a beautiful walk and while watching an exultant sunrise or sunset. Or, lie down and take deep breaths until you can almost see your cells sparkling. Think back to a time when you felt *most alive, most truly yourself.*

When did you feel and live most free of outer influences? Where were you in your life when you were closest to being and living the life that most closely felt like your own? What times most closely seemed to fit your picture or vision of how you saw your life? What music were you listening to then?

When those times come back to you, travel to them. While it's not good to dwell in the past, you can transcend the illusion of time to recapture what is of value from special times. So, as you travel to a particular time, remember all kinds of associations: places you visited, things you did, smells, popular music at the time, and people who contributed to your feelings of aliveness. When feelings come up, follow them. Relive those times. If you keep returning and returning to a particular time, a time your heart yearns toward, really allow yourself to relive it. Let those special feelings come up, and remember the promises your life held.

You are an individual who is absolutely unique. Your uniqueness is spectacular. When you are most fully living that which is *true* for you, you are expressing and exalting Spirit. You are engendering *self-realization*.

The whole idea of treading a spiritual path is to progress in *self-realization*. Think of your life as a rosebud, opening through the years. As it comes more fully into flower, it opens to its beauty and truth. Self-realization is that process by which you open into the truth and fulfill the positive possibilities of your existence. Thus, self-realization is that process by which you (a) express your uniqueness, (b) pursue those paths that call to you, (c) become the best *you* in every sphere of life, (d) grow in spirituality, developing all the virtues, and (e) realize that *you are the soul*, in essence, a drop of the divine ocean of love.

As a human being, for now possessing the inestimable gift of a human life, your first and most essential duty is to pursue self-realization. More than all your worldly and familial duties, your duty is to be your true self and utilize your life for spiritual growth.

It is so easy to lose sight of this fact and get gridlocked, just making it back and forth between your daily destinations. That's why you want to take advantage of a vacation to shift your consciousness from its habitual commute. Your consciousness can be refreshed from its customary thoughts, imaginary confrontations, and stolen fantasies.

Thus, a vacation is an opportunity for rest, release, renewal, remembrance, and re-energizing. It's an opportunity for capturing a clear perspective and coming back to your everyday world with keener priorities, committed to pursuing your first duty. These clearer priorities and your renewed energy need to be supported by firm commitment, a commitment that will push you through and lift you over barriers. Getting past barriers is aided by inner knowing and will. What can help? Taking *another* vacation.

# FOUR

# Daily Disciplines for a Spiritual Foundation

# Take a Vacation, Part Two

*I*f you wish, there's a way you can take a vacation whenever you want. With this vacation, you don't have to make arrangements to have your work finished, have your mail held, or make additional umpteen arrangements for your house, pets, and children. And, oh, yes—this vacation is free. What's more, this can be a vacation in the profoundest sense. Here's how to do it.

## ❖ Activity ❖

Find a time when you won't be disturbed. If you have children, a pet, a partner, or a parent who expects unlimited access, ensure that for this time, they'll be self-sufficient. Turn off the volume on your phones and answering machines. Darken the room and even close the window, if you wish. Sit yourself in a comfortable way. Be relaxed and comfortable, almost lazy. Whether you sit on a cushion on the floor or on a big easy chair, it's important to be comfortable enough so you're not fighting with your body, yet not so comfortable that you're lulled to sleep.

Now, close your eyes and just be where your attention is. Focus on your center of consciousness, the place inside you where you're aware. Usually, it's above your eyes an inch or so, inside a bit. Choose a phrase or affirmation or mantra to repeat at this center of consciousness. Or, choose a name for your Higher Power. Repeat this with love and one-pointedness. One-pointedness means to continuously focus all conscious activity toward that one point. Keep repeating it and repeating it.

Each time you notice your attention has slipped, use your phrase to bring your attention back. You'll find your mind playing out scenes of conversations and confrontations, obsessing on problems, fantasizing about sex and secret wishes. It's just doing its job. Your mind loves doing its job, for *it loves going out and out and out*. Now, each time you notice that your mind has gone out and you're not repeating at your center of consciousness, bring it back. Don't get upset. Just bring back your mind again and again. *And again.* Keep concentrating. Keep repeating. Let yourself transcend all physical awareness to open to the finer things inside. You can do it, for what you're doing is *meditation*.

*Meditation* is a means by which we center our attention. The purpose of meditation is not to make you think better, although it will. It's best not to meditate with the purpose of solving your problems, although that is often a side benefit. Look at meditation as taking a vacation away from your problems. Thus, when you're concentrated and meditating, your mind is not obsessively churning over its worries. Rather, you're centering your consciousness more and more in the place of inspiration so that, without thinking about problems, their solutions will come automatically. You will just know what to do.

Nor should you meditate to gain special powers. Meditate to respond to an inner pull. Meditate for self-realization. Meditate as your best prayer for God. Meditate, meditate, meditate to bring your Self closer to the Supreme Being, that infinite, eternal ocean of love.

The most profound rest, the greatest renewal, and the best progress toward self-realization can come from meditation. Meditation is simply vacating your doors to the sensory world—your eyes, ears, mouth, sex organs, and so on—and focusing your attention on your spiritual door. That spiritual door, or single eye or third eye, is a place between and above your eyes. It is the place to which your consciousness, when properly centered and concentrated, can withdraw.

Through proper meditation, we can withdraw from the world, vacate our bodies, and experience true freedom. Not only is it physically deeply relaxing and healing but meditation is also the foundation of spiritual practice. In meditation, we connect with our higher Self, moving ever closer to our Higher Power. Through meditation, we invoke the mercy and grace of God. It's a way of asking for remission for our trespasses, those thoughts and actions we've committed that have carried us away from God. It's a way of knocking for admittance into the Court of the Lord. That's not an idle statement. Through proper meditation, we can embark on a true vacation, vacating the illusory world of time and sensation and entering the truer spirit worlds, those many mansions within that God has made available to each of us. Until we have seen them firsthand, we can only imagine their vastly superior beauty.

These finer, higher worlds do not exist in the everyday physical plane. Unfortunately, NASA can't send a probe to transmit photographs. But Saints, humans who have realized their full potential in consciousness, have spoken and written throughout time of this higher existence, directly and in parable. Those who have not possessed the knowledge of or the ability to enter the inner finer spiritual realm have suppressed that this is a possibility that God has made available to all humans. Yet, meditation is so simple that anyone can do it. It's best undertaken with the right teacher.

Meditation is your God-given birthright and, with practice, the best vacation you'll ever take. The true benefit of this vacation is that, as you meditate daily, you'll begin to vacate your old way of being and find yourself in a place where you experience more peace, focus, energy, forgiveness, love, and quiet joy.

# Adopt a Spiritual Practice and Follow It Faithfully

Spiritual love is awakened by God's grace and spiritual practice. Demonstrations to your Higher Power for special favor, no matter how demanding or deserving, will not cause that grace to be showered. God gives as that Power wills. You have but to do your duty, your best.

If you study the lives of those who have attained great spirituality, you will find that they have also been great disciples of saints and spiritual teachings. The hallmark of a devoted disciple is *discipline*. The words are virtually identical. ***Discipline*** is marshaling your will and *continuing* to apply yourself. Your practice becomes your foundation.

A key thing that you can do to develop your spirituality is to adopt a practice and follow it faithfully with discipline. For this, choose something that you're ready and willing to integrate into your life as part of the foundation of your active spiritual life. Thus, it can be daily meditation, daily prayer, volunteering on a regular basis at a charitable organization, curbing your anger and cultivating sweetness, or exploring the richness of solitude. Other practices you could choose may be reading some part of a spiritual book daily, diverting to a worthy cause money that's been feeding a bad habit, opening your heart and turning to God during your work commute, or catching your thoughts when they rush to negative judgments. Right now, choose your spiritual practice.

If you haven't picked something, stop. Give yourself the luxury of choosing something you'd really love to do. Something that will feed your soul. You know what it is. Whatever you choose, integrate it firmly into your life and, initially, use some means to remember to do it so that it becomes a part of your foundation, a regular focus of your life, actually part of you. You may wish to schedule it on a calendar or organizer. You may wish to leave a self-stick note on a lamp or mirror to remind you. You may wish to write your new practice on a sheet of paper and post it with magnets on your refrigerator. Perhaps you've really taken the plunge and are substituting your new spiritual practice for an unnecessary, unproductive activity that you habitually engaged in. If so, every time that habitual urge comes up, it may serve as a reminder.

The first step is simply doing the discipline. Don't let procrastination get the best of you. The next step is simply doing it *again*, just when you planned to. You have the power to follow through. Don't let yourself get side-tracked. You have all the time you need. And if you feel that you simply don't have the time, why not prove to yourself that you have the power to make the time? The next virtue will support you in this.

Perhaps you have the time, but you'd rather watch TV. Be aware that your lower mind is pleasure-loving and resists discipline, and through discipline comes achievement and bliss. You can choose either a Lean Cuisine heated in your microwave or a sumptuous meal that transports you to an exquisite place. The choice is yours. You are the cook, and if you want the latter meal, you'll have to be responsible for all the preparations.

Very few of us were born millionaires. Most of us have to work to achieve our spiritual wealth, and laziness may be the main obstacle you'll have to surmount. Another name for laziness is "I'll get around to it." And don't forget: "Later," "Tomorrow," "I don't feel like it," and "There's always another day." Or, you may simply not remember.

It's up to you to decide whether you want to continue climbing your mountain or whether you want to camp out with your remote on your recliner, where it's comfortable. The antidote to laziness is conviction, responsibility, and regularity. You must form the conviction to inculcate the discipline in your consciousness and life. Remember the virtues desire and intention? Apply them. Taking responsibility for integrating discipline into your life is autonomy. Practicing discipline with regularity is practice.

To achieve this, employ whatever means suit you. The important thing is to faithfully practice on a regular basis. If it's helping at a charitable organization on Wednesday evening, keep your calendar free on Wednesday, arrange matters at work so that you can always leave on time on Wednesday, and *show up* at the organization ready to work. If it's exploring spiritual literature last thing before you go to sleep, put your current book on your bed, and don't go to bed so tired that you can't read. Be ready and in good condition to discern the spiritual truths of your reading.

Enjoy the discipline that is providing the conditions for new growth. Remember that regularity leads to integration into your life, and that leads to further growth. But for your tender seedlings to grow, you must always be on the lookout for weeds and pests.

# For Three Days, Make a List of Everything You Do

Your new spiritual discipline is like a tender seedling that, if not cared for and cultivated, can get overgrown by weeds. Rampant desires and demands are continually sprouting up to complicate your life and overshadow what is truly of value.

## ❖ Activity ❖

For the next three days, list everything you do. Be specific. List phone calls, what you read, TV shows you watch, what music you listen to, and so on. At the end of the three days, code each item as follows: "E" for essential, "P" for preferable, and "N" for nonessential. Be ruthless as you consider whether each thing is something actually essential for your life, work, and family; preferable; or nonessential and easily eliminated. Then identify the most time-consuming nonessential activity and stop it. By doing so, you are *simplifying and prioritizing*.

If we don't regularly weed our gardens, the tender shoots of our spirituality are quickly overgrown. By *simplifying and prioritizing*, we're cutting back on the nonessential demands of the world and our desires and clearing space to facilitate our growth and flowering. This is an everyday discipline that we need to follow if we are to develop our spirituality. We need to give priority to our spiritual work as we simplify our life. Our material needs are basic: food, clothing, and shelter. But we expand them and aggrandize them to the point where we're no longer satisfying needs but running after rampant desires. How can we strive one-pointedly toward fulfilling our purpose in life if we're running out of breath trying to keep up with our desires?

A leading cause of stress is simply having too much to do. We get scattered, drained, and deflected from our goals. A solution to this is just to eliminate the nonessential. Think of elimination as positive and necessary: You're weeding your garden to enable your goals to flourish. Since spirituality is most easily postponed and not tended to, eliminating other activities to concentrate on your spiritual practices is essential. An alternative for some items is to delegate or pay someone else to get the work done.

Many of us are terrified of space. If our calendars aren't full, if one evening is open, something is terribly wrong and we take action to fill it up. Or, we get through our lives by getting from one television show to the next. If, somehow, the VCR gets misprogrammed, it's a major catastrophe. Everything that we do to avoid facing ourselves we do consciously or unconsciously to deaden the pain. But we're really deadening ourselves. To eliminate the plastic pabulum, make open space, and then direct yourself in a spiritual direction takes tremendous courage. And you have it.

# Review Your Dealings in the Workplace for Honesty

*O*nce you are following a discipline, simplifying your life, and bringing spiritual elements into your life, the quality and basis of that life comes into clearer relief.

❖ **Exercise** ❖

Close your eyes and open your imagination. First, wonder about what your conscience is. It is your sense of right, which guides you away from wrong. Now, think of your conscience as a piece of glass.

Visualize a large glass slate that's perfectly clean and clear. It's so incredibly clear that you can see through your conscience to divine truth. What happens if you cheat someone? A dark mark is etched on the board. What happens if you sell snake oil at $50 a bottle, but it's not worth the 30 cents you paid for it nor is it snake oil nor does it do any of the things you promise? For each sale, your glass is gouged with a deep dark stroke.

If you're a student who doesn't work, apply the principles in this section to your school. If you're not a student and you don't work, instead of the workplace, consider people and institutions with which you have dealings, particularly monetary dealings.

## ❖ Continuing Exercise ❖

Now, visualize the light of your Higher Power shining on all the deep gouges and dirty smudges on the glass of your conscience. As the light shines on each one, what is revealed about dishonest things you've done? With that light shining from mark to mark, review those things that are dug into your conscience. For every violation, see how it affected you and those others involved. Take responsibility for your actions, and if possible, resolve to correct the damage and forgive yourself. If you can't correct the damage, resolve to act with higher consciousness in the future so as not to cause similar damage, then forgive yourself.

Dishonesty can work like a dark plague, clouding the clarity of your conscience so that you're not even aware of the dishonesty nor of your conscience. Unbeknownst to you, you can carry the hard spores of dishonesty, spreading them within yourself as well as within others.

We are all part of God and connected to one another. God is truth. When we're dishonest, it's as though we are severing our connection with our Source. But every action, every thought, is on some level known. Nothing is done in a vacuum; everything we do either adds light or digs a dark groove.

Similarly, whatever we eat and drink becomes part of us. The way in which we earn our food is transmitted in that very food and absorbed by us. We absorb it both physically and vibrationally. Many are the stories of saints who politely refused rich repasts offered by those who had earned their wealth dishonestly, while accepting lovingly the simple meals offered by poor-but-honest people. Food will carry negativity when obtained dishonestly through exploitation, force, breaking the law, unnecessary begging, chicanery, cheating, or any shenanigans that we rationalize, in any way, while taking advantage of others. The very vibration of the food is altered to reflect the nature in which it was obtained. When you serve it to your family and friends or eat it yourself, and it's ingested and digested, its darkness spreads.

Therefore, a prime component in building a good and solid

spiritual foundation is ***honest living***. This daily discipline has a subtle-yet-profound effect on your ability to progress spiritually. Food that is earned by honest means favorably affects the quality of your thoughts and facilitates the imbibing of virtues. ***Honest living*** shows a respect for the life you have been given and a faith in your Higher Power as Provider. It's both an act of surrender and a joining with a Greater Power to live nobly. Rather than discount the importance of honest living, why not take a moment for the following exercise?

## ❖ Exercise ❖

Review your dealings in the workplace for honesty. Close your eyes and visualize the glass of your conscience. How clear is it? What smudges, streaks, gouges, and dirt cloud the glass? Form and concentrate your intent to have a clear conscience. Now, visualize your own bottle of glass cleaner, which you use to clean the window to your inner light. Spray the cleaner on the window of your conscience to loosen the dirt. Wipe off the first layer and review the basis of how you get money to buy food and to live. Are you living off others or the public when you have the capability to work? Are you profiting from harmful goods or substances? In what way are you exploiting the poor, the young, the old, the less sophisticated?

Spray and wipe off your glass again, and remember people with whom you've had dealings. What do you feel uneasy about? In those dealings, what did you misrepresent? Whom did you overcharge? Where did you take unfair advantage? Did you switch goods or hide inferior elements? What distortions or lies are interwoven in your dealings? How have you fudged on your time reports? On what promises did you renege? Review your dealings in the workplace for all these elements and more.

Decide what you must do to clean up your act and imbue all your dealings with honesty. Resolve to do whatever it takes, spray your cleaner yet again, and wipe off the glass until it is sparkling clean. Open your eyes slowly and focus on things around you. If so moved, write what dishonesty came up and what you will do to right things.

Once you earn your livelihood on an entirely honest basis where no one is treated unfairly, you'll feel lighter, with more energy and with focused inner purpose to bring more spirituality into your life. When you add the fundamental daily discipline of honest living to your foundation, you're better able to go out into the world and practice spirituality successfully.

# FIVE

# *Practicing*
# *Spirituality*
# *in Your World*

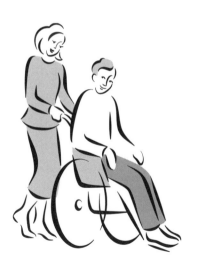

# Make an Agreement and Keep It

One sign of a stalled life is a life strewn with broken agreements. People who habitually make and break agreements spend most of their time avoiding or dealing with the results of their broken agreements. One hallmark of powerful people, people who are focused and able to proceed forward with life, is that they're able to give their word and keep it.

## ❖ Activity ❖

Make an agreement and keep it. You may choose to make an agreement to keep an agreement, vow, or commitment you previously made. Look clearly at your life and determine just what it is you must do to get your life more firmly in focus. Have confidence in your knowingness of where to start. Here are examples of the types of agreements you may make.

1. If mundane day-to-day agreements are a particular problem, if, for instance, you're habitually late or you don't make promised calls, then agree to meet or call the person you most often let down. This may not seem that important, but if you can't follow through on a simple phone call, how will you ever begin to triumph over the wayward tendencies of your lower mind that habitually lead you away from God and your deserved happiness?

2. If you've made a vow of monogamy and you've been having an affair or fantasizing about every good-looking man or woman who crosses your path, your agreement may be to remake the vow of monogamy. You will exercise newfound strength as you struggle to keep it.

3. The agreement may also be just with yourself. If you've been thinking about taking a special class, such as a singing or athletic class, now is the time to make the agreement with yourself, sign up, and attend each session. Or perhaps an important relationship is faltering

and you've been wanting to talk to the other person about it. Sweeping your intended communication under the rug will just make you more likely to trip up. Honestly look at the relationship and see how it isn't mutually furthering your aliveness, healing, and love. Once you know just how the relationship isn't right and what you need to communicate to the other person to enable it to work, make the agreement with yourself to set up a special time with that person, by a certain date, to meet.

No matter how gruelingly difficult completing these are, you will prosper as a result. When you make an agreement and keep it, you make your word the law of the universe. When you make an agreement and keep it, you are speaking and living the *truth*. Why is truth so important? Wonder about it.

God is truth. ***Truthfulness*** is the virtue that is the beginning and end of our spirituality. To achieve something in spirituality, you must make ***truthfulness*** the fabric of your everyday life. A key to developing spirituality is to hone to the truth in your thoughts, speech, conduct, and spiritual practice. If your life is based in large part on untruth, living and expressing the truth may initially seem bitter, while resorting to lies, deceptions, ploys, and pretenses may seem seductively comfortable or even right. Remember, it is relatively easy to rationalize your actions. But dealing in untruth is like tossing a glass ball. Soon, you must juggle several, then more, and eventually they come crashing down, shattering at your feet.

Without truthfulness as a rock-solid foundation of a relationship, both people ultimately suffer. Yet, it's crucial to be truthful in a way that does not injure another's feelings; for when we live in truth, we also show compassion and mercy for others. In doing so, we speak from the heart, feeling respect for and kinship with the other person's divinity and human struggles.

Where there is truthfulness, there is no hypocrisy, lying, cheating, deceit, cunning, fear, or broken promises. A person who is truthful is confident and attracts the confidence of others. A person who lives truth has a calm mind and their attention more readily centers on God. A person who practices truth in the world—in their thoughts, speech, actions, and relationships—imbues the world with God, thus uplifting those in their sphere.

# Choose Four Principles, Own Them, and Follow Them

*Y*ou may wish to practice truth in the world, and a great support in doing so is being anchored to principles that you know to be true. In today's world, where anything goes, where just about anything passes for spirituality, and where the most curious experts purvey soul in tantalizing ways, a powerful boon is to have guidelines by which you can always find your spiritual center. Being grounded in your spiritual center will help you attract all those who can support you on your true path. This will also help you withstand onslaughts from all the well-meaning teachers and helpful leeches who beat a path to your door to urge you to try the latest fixes of soul.

Spiritual principles can also save you during your own wanderings. Just when you think that you know where you stand, sorting through the babble (that's the only thing you finally realize you recognize from some expert's *Tour de Soul* that you signed up for), you can easily find yourself sinking in quicksand with nary a tree's branch within grasp. If you have principles that you own, you may not stray into such a predicament. Try this activity if you're interested in forming a base that will serve you as an initial foundation.

❖ **Activity** ❖

Use any method for choosing four principles. If you're stumped, this may work for you. On a clean sheet of paper, make a list titled "What I Know to Be True." Write as quickly as you can, without censoring anything. Write another list, titled "What Will Move Me into the Light." Write like lightning. Scan your lists. Are there any items you could form into principles? Ideally, these principles will support your growing spirituality and also challenge your unfolding as a human.

Here's an example of a set of four principles for someone who has particular issues with gossip, honesty, drugs, and money.

1. Do not intentionally hurt another person by word or deed.

2. Live honestly.

3. Take drugs only as prescribed by a doctor to promote health.

4. Use money responsibly and consciously.

Here's another set of four principles for someone who has particular issues with negative thoughts, anger, workaholism, and self-centeredness.

1. Employ positive thinking.

2. Work out anger constructively.

3. Spend time wisely.

4. Give of myself to family and friends.

You'll notice that some of the principles are expressed as warnings to refrain from certain behavior. They are to be *your* daily disciplines that foster the growth of your spiritual crop. Think of these principles as weeding, pruning, fertilizing, and staking your crop. Thus, choosing principles that are true for you will allow the tender seedlings of your spirituality to grow and flourish as you channel your energy.

If you wish to review a complete range of principles, one source you may turn to is *Spiritual Revolution: A Seeker's Guide; 52 Powerful Principles for Your Mind and Soul* by Michael Goddart. This book illuminates all the foundations needed for a spiritual life.

In choosing your four principles, you'll want to explore what they really mean to you. Wonder about all their ramifications. How will adopting them affect you on a practical day-to-day basis? How will they change the way you feel about yourself? How will they awaken your Self, your higher mind and soul? Feel what resonates with you. Which principles feel just right for you now and will continue to from now on?

Choose your four principles and write them down.

It's one thing to choose principles to live by. It's another thing to *own* your principles and make them part of your everyday life. To do this, start by making the principles into specific agreements or promises. The actual agreement should be something that you need to work on for your growth, something that may be challenging, and yet something that you can attain and maintain with resolve. The specifics can evolve and deepen with your growth.

If you're not clear about how you want to express your principles as agreements, you may find it helpful to take a walk. While taking a walk, you may find yourself naturally inspired and come to know what it is you must do. Thus, for the first set of examples, the person could resolve the following.

1. I agree not to intentionally hurt another person by word or deed. Specifically, I will not engage in gossip that is hurtful or negative in any degree. Nor will I spread rumors or make up stories about people. I will concentrate on my own business.

2. I agree to live honestly and not take any money or supplies from work. Nor will I take anything from stores, no matter how much I want to or feel I deserve to or how inconsequential the stealing seems.

3. I agree to take only those drugs prescribed by a doctor to promote my health. Thus, I will not take any kind of diet pill nor any recreational drugs, no matter how harmless they seem or how much I feel I need them at the time.

4. I agree to use money responsibly and consciously and buy only those things that I truly need and want for myself. I will put aside 15 percent of my take-home pay to pay off credit cards; and I will keep track of my credit card purchases, limiting them to $500 a month. I will not buy expensive gifts with an agenda of wanting to impress someone or "buy" love.

The second set of examples could lead the person to resolve the following.

1. I agree to do my best to change my focus when I find that it's on what is wrong or lacking. Rather than always seeing the glass as half-empty, I will see it as half-full, *and* remembering all my bountiful gifts from God, it may become full. When my mind gets on a negative treadmill about what is not right in my life, I will pull back, break that cycle of thinking, and affirm everything I am doing to improve my life.

2. I agree to work out my anger constructively and not verbally attack any family members. Even when my anger truly seems warranted, I will accept other people's humanity, be objective, and practice spiritual maturity. Also, when drivers drive me crazy, I will rise above the urge to vent road rage, and I will accept their human limitations and practice forgiveness.

3. I agree to catch myself when my workaholism takes over. I will hug myself and acknowledge my misguided attempts to fill what is lacking in my life with work. Appreciating the fact that I have only a certain amount of time

in this life, I will simplify and prioritize that very day so that I take time out for my Self, doing one of the simple spiritual things that reconnects me.

4. I will cultivate an awareness of when my ego—my small self—totally takes over. When I realize that just about every thought, sentence, and deed is wrapped up in me, myself, and I, I will reach out to a friend or family member with whom I've been out of touch. I will truly listen to what is going on in that person's life and, if needed, do something that week to help.

These are promises you make to your Self, to anchor your Self at your spiritual center and to encourage the growth you are seeking. To really own these agreements, write them out and keep them in a place where you can refer to them regularly. Referring to these agreements or promises regularly will support you in following these principles.

Following your principles, expressed as specific agreements designed for your benefit, is the third part of making them your foundation. Following and keeping your agreements in heart, mind, and deed will give you *obedience*. *Obedience* is a gift you give your Self to keep your Self centered and doing those things that are truly good for you. Thus, it's a prime example of love in action. True obedience is sourced in your conscience, in what you know to be true and good for you. If it is merely imposed from without by an external authority, it will be deleterious to you, creating internal conflicts.

If you wish to be obedient to an external authority, you must first accept that the authority possesses a greater wisdom for your welfare; otherwise, how can you begin to own and obey the rules that you have accepted? It is always best to practice obedience to rules, guidelines, principles, or agreements to which you are wholly aligned. They also need to be for your spiritual betterment. If this is the case, you are following the formula for the best progress.

If following your principles starts to feel like drudgery, like a straitjacket, like you're being barred from good times, you need to examine the spirit in which you made the agreements and what it is that you truly need and want from life. Also examine your relationship to them. If you are not realigning yourself with your principles and agreements, you may need to assess the appropriateness of the agreements and where you are now. You are bound to encounter resistance as you go through life getting pulled in different directions. Remember, the aim of this activity is to practice obedience. Your mind has a broad range, from lazy and low-pleasure-loving to noble, sacrificing, and refined. The battle is within yourself. Conduct it with determination and forgiveness. You may be expecting immediate perfection and then judging yourself harshly when you don't meet the mark. If you fall, refrain from all judgments. And if you fall, fall towards the light, with your eyes on the prize. Thus, you will keep your objective always in view.

These agreements, which are expressions of the spiritual principles you have adopted, are practicing spirituality in your world. They are nurturing your crop. They aren't the crop itself. Tending the crop is attending to your spiritual practice and doing things to inculcate the virtues and strengths. Harvesting the crop is realizing love in your life and unfolding to your Self. The crops improve gradually from year to year; know that you will need to cultivate your field for many a season. Know also that bad weather will come to test your resources. At times, it can even destroy your crop, but being obedient helps you *return* to your good practices and can save that crop.

Being obedient to your principles is strengthening your foundation for a spiritual life. But life is always changing; you're always changing. You may find it best to avoid being so rigid that you can't adjust to what is appropriate and right in the moment. While you want your foundation to be ever so solid and strong, don't think of it as a single, flat, rigid structure, like a thick concrete floor. Think of it as a living, breathing, forgiving, multi-layered, fluid structure that supports you always. Think of your foundation in the plural, as *foundations* that are viable, developing and deepening in profundity as your spirituality intensifies.

The purification process is a slow process, and the wayward tendencies of the mind are powerful, indeed. The mind is changeable and fickle. Trust your principles. Your obedience expresses that trust. When your mind goes off a deep end, when waves of the world crash in on you, your obedience will anchor you to your foundations.

# Get a Daily Weather Report

Weather is constantly changing and affecting our lives. Sometimes, it's overcast; next, it may be sunny and cool; sometimes, big storms come and it rains and rains, creating floods. And one day, you may be out walking, unawares, when a hailstorm unleashes a deluge, bonking you on the head. When weather is unpleasant, you must put up with it, dress accordingly, and do your best to adapt to it. If you really dislike gloomy weather and usually feel gloomy when thick clouds are blocking the sun, you're allowing an external force to order your mood. This is giving up your power.

## ❖ Activity ❖

To be prepared, obtain a daily weather report. Now that toll-free information telephone lines are common, you can listen to weather reports from cities around the world, so obtain another report or two. Usually, that weather is different; what one part of the world is going through, your part is not. Let this remind you that while you're putting up with yet another day of heavy overcast, other people are dealing with freezing cold or hot, muggy weather.

While not a sure prediction, a weather report helps you prepare for what is coming and serves as a reminder that you must adjust to changing external conditions. It's not the other way; if you want a sunny Sunday for an outing, rain clouds will not, out of deference to you, avoid your picnic.

Like weather, the winds of life are always shifting, bringing you different weather. Some days, nothing seems to go right; or you have too much to do and too many people waiting for you to get back to them; or no one calls and you seem to have disappeared from the planet; or a family member takes ill and needs you; or someone you were depending on doesn't come through; or you feel out of sorts and come down with a cold. Life is always blowing hot and cold and everything in between.

If you're anxious about life, if you're easily buffeted by the changing weather of life, you need to develop one-pointedness and determination. To live with the realization that life is always changing—that sunny days are replaced by overcast days, which are replaced by days of thick ground fog, which are blown away by gale-force winds—is to keep yourself focused on your goal.

### ❖ Exercise ❖

If you're used to getting a weather report at a particular time in the morning or evening, join that with a report of your life. Check in with yourself and report what is happening. Perhaps, today, someone snapped at you for no good reason. Or, you kept daydreaming and got hardly anything done. Maybe you felt lousy. Or, maybe it was such a crazy day that it felt as though it were raining people.

Whatever your day, report to yourself on it, *objectively, without judgment*. If you're unhappy about things that happened or did not happen, remember a time—and surely there was one—when the situation was quite different. Know that these unhappy conditions will pass.

Sometimes, in the summer, it can be unseasonably cold. Unlike the person who refuses to put on a sweater for the cold, because it's summer and it's supposed to be warm, learn how to adjust to the shifting weather of life. Happiness resides in *adjusting* to life.

*Adjusting* to life, emotionally, mentally, and physically, is the spiritual virtue that enables you to give the world its due and roll with its punches while you hold to your spiritual center. It's being flexible while operating from your viable foundations, responding to the craziness of the world with maturity and practicality.

Adjusting your attitude and taking practical measures to regain your balance and direction, rather than getting stuck in a reaction of upset, is crucial if you are to successfully make headway and practice spirituality in the world. For instance, if you only meditate when you feel inspiration or when there's absolute quiet, how much meditation will you accomplish? Thus, if you have an agreement of daily meditation but someone is blaring music right at your special time, rather than run out of the house in a rage, you could choose to adjust and either put on white noise, meditate at a different time, or concentrate so well that you rise above the noise. When you adjust, you can go through the world with equanimity, balance, and one-pointedness in achieving your goals. That is because adjusting is not giving up or fighting, but shifting your attitude and mode of operation, *keeping your sure, strong center*.

Adjusting entails an acceptance of and respect for reality — both the physical reality of the world and the reality of your makeup and those people in your world. Adjusting to the weather and the weather of your life is, in a sense, an austerity. An austerity is physical or mental hardship for purification to bring you closer to

God. The idea is to undergo the hardship while remaining one-pointed on God.

Undergoing an austerity for the sake of suffering to gain purity is counterproductive, for, ultimately, the mind will rebel. You must give it something sweeter. So, rather than using enforced rituals, such as long-term fasting or exposing yourself to harsh elements, for so-called spiritual development, it is more effective to start with centering your attention on your Higher Power. Then, attend to your worldly work and family responsibilities as well as making the best time possible for your spiritual practices. Rather than strip to your underwear and sit out day after day under the broiling sun to gain spirituality (and quite possibly skin cancer), why not dress sensibly, according to the weather, use a skin lotion with a high sun protection factor, and go about your business doing good, while keeping your attention on your spiritual work? The weather of life is difficult enough without adding to it by needless suffering or resisting reality. That's why adjusting to life, rather than expecting life to change to your preferences, is a necessary booster to developing your spirituality.

Don't expect perfection and things to go the way you want them to when it comes to people, business, your prospects, and your social life. When things don't go according to your desires, when the weather of life is foul, be creative and consider what may be the higher reasons why this is happening and why you must adjust. Perhaps it's to gain forbearance, patience, inner strength, flexibility, or the ability to withhold criticism while serving as a loving model.

## ❖ Exercise ❖

What is the situation that is now making you most unhappy? Is it that you're lonely? The behavior of a loved one? Your inability to progress in a career or to know just what work you wish to do? Mentally step outside yourself and look at yourself with loving benevolence. Let's say that the one thing you're most unhappy about is the lack of people in your life, despite your good efforts. You finally admit it: You're lonely. Say mentally to yourself, "I accept my loneliness." Now, rise to your higher Self, or imagine that you are doing so, and look down on yourself, see your loneliness, and feel compassion and love. Let yourself know what the *higher reasons* are for your loneliness. If this doesn't currently feel attainable, let yourself *consider* the possible higher reasons.

Perhaps you have a huge amount of work to get done at this time, and people would be too great a distraction. Perhaps you're not well, and you need to concentrate your energies on healing. Perhaps you're going through a transition, and the people who have been in your life are not a good influence. Perhaps your thoughts are flat-out negative: "Women just suck you in and use you up." "Men are abusive jerks." "People just want to take advantage of me." If your mind is spewing out negative thoughts like these, you may need to adjust your thinking and think the positive. For instance, "Women wish to empower me and contribute to my spirituality."

Perhaps you're going through an austere spiritual period in which you need to experience that you can't look for happiness in people and you need to turn your attention to your Higher Power within. You can come to know why something is causing you unhappiness and adjust to it in the present moment. You can adjust to it while you bide your time, knowing that things are coming to you for your spiritual benefit, always at the appropriate time. Once you gain even a little insight and let go and adjust, those unhappy conditions will shift. Even if feeling that you know why things are coming to you a certain way *eludes* you, you can still let go and adjust and find happiness in your spiritual center.

Keep your intentions strong and one-pointed. For instance, repeat, "I easily attract loving, spiritual, empathetic people in my life," while knowing and emotionally accepting that everything can go against your wishes and very well may *and* that there is a higher reason for this. This is developing spiritual maturity. Exhibiting spiritual maturity through making all kinds of adjustments will help you accrue great power.

Americans, in particular, can believe in their mastery over nature, other people, and events. But to what extent can you really change externals? Can you make a loved one stop smoking? No, the change must come from within. Can you stop a friend from feeling self-pity? No, that change must come from within. Can you go to the people department at your local department store to pick out the perfect spouse and a great set of flawless friends? Oh, if only life were so easy. Happiness resides in adjusting to each situation, while remaining one-pointed on your goals. That is the austerity worth performing. When times are hard, when you're being buffeted by the strong winds of life, tell yourself, "This too, shall pass," make whatever adjustments you can to deal effectively with the situation, and continue to work toward your goals.

# Spend a Day in Slow Motion

When you don't go at your own speed, it is difficult to flow with your spirituality. You become exhausted from cramming too much into your all-too-meager days. You rush around trying to do three, four, five things at once.

Remember: "To hurry is satanic." How can you attend to your spirituality if you're doing so much that you can barely handle everything?

With all our advanced technologies, we need never be separated from that phone call, fax, or e-mail that we need to get this second. In getting overscheduled and hurrying through life with a voracious appetite for getting things done, we're working smarter and staying in communication ever more effectively, but are we staying in communication with our Self? One telecommunication company promises to be "your true voice." How externalized have we become that we believe this subversive, smarmy pitch claiming that, by signing up, we get not merely clearer speech but also, more important, the true voice of real communication, community, and a rosy life? And how disconnected have we become that the only voices of which we're aware are our physical voices? What about the *true* voice of our Self?

Technology is advancing at an exponential rate, and its insidious effect in our culture can be to divorce us from our Self. What would have been astoundingly quick two years ago is now intolerably slow, an insult to our identities as masters of technology — or, at least, master "dummies" of technology. Technology commands an increasingly dominant place in our lives; and our worldly work demands higher and higher productivity. Not only do we more readily lose sight of what matters now *and* in the long run but even if we are lucky to schedule some time for our spiritual development, we may expect immediate results or pursue it so frenetically that we become more stressed than we were when we began.

Once, a disciple and teacher were traveling in a small car through a village. The lanes became narrower, crammed with more bustling people and every manner of conveyance. Their progress was slowed and slowed until, finally, they found themselves stopped behind a bullock that was so huge that it was larger than their car. There was no way around the bullock, and it seemed to not be moving forward at all. They waited behind the towering animal, and finally, he seemed to budge infinitesimally ahead. Exasperated, the disciple complained, "Can't we honk the horn to get him moving?"; whereupon, the teacher said, with a genial nod, "He knows how to move at his right speed."

## ❖ Activity ❖

Spend a day in slow motion. Plan ahead and really dedicate a whole day to moving in slow motion. When you're moving about your house, going to work, eating, and so on, *slow . . . down*. Whatever your speed, concentrate on cutting it in half. Remember to breathe. Find your most comfortable, slow rhythm and breathe slowly and fully as you go about each task, happily remembering your Higher Power when you do so. As you finish one thing and take off for another, you'll probably forget that you promised yourself to spend the day in slow motion. Just remind yourself. Keep reminding yourself and slowing down. Pat yourself on the back for taking this time to relax and discover your natural rhythms, and enjoy this new sense of being.

Moving in slow motion is beginning to balance all the times that you hurried and pushed and strained and rushed. Some of us operate more or less in permanent fight-or-flight mode. We struggle with one after another urgency or deadline until everything becomes a race to beat the clock. Even a simple trip to a hair-styling appointment becomes a race and a stress. This is not living. This is not promoting our health, well-being, and connection to our Higher Power. We've let ourselves be dominated by false urgency of circumstance, losing our center and natural tempo.

What is the spiritual virtue you wish to call forth here? Finding your right speed and rhythm, according to circumstance, and following that is maintaining *equipoise*. *Equipoise* helps you keep your head above water in the swirling undertows of the world. Equipoise is a means to creating present mindfulness and not losing your attention. Present mindfulness and attention are key resources of spirituality that require constant development, yet are all too easily forgotten.

Many of us are lost in a whirlwind of activity, speeding along at full throttle, just skimming the surface of life. At this breakneck speed, it is easy to miss the signs and scenery along the way that are there actually for our spiritual growth. But our eyes are always straining outside ourselves on some distant destination. If we manage to keep going, speeding along, as soon as we reach or even near our destination (a worldly goal that promises to deliver happiness to us), another far-off, distant point takes its place and our attention. So, we take off again with greater urgency, missing the signs and the opportunities until we crash.

Then, a back injury, a broken relationship, a major illness, or whatever challenge we're given will command our attention so that we must adjust to practice equipoise. Without critical adjusting to achieve the much needed equipoise, the situation will grow worse and worse.

We are toddlers in this game of spirituality. A Saint is able to move at a seemingly breakneck speed yet maintain perfect equipoise, with their attention wholly absorbed in God. For now, just be happy to take slow, easy steps. Take one step at a time in slow motion, maintaining your attention in God. If you have a repetition or saying that centers your attention, you'll find it much easier to repeat it while you are moving in slow motion. Concentrating on where you are now, dwelling in the means, not the end, is the key to gathering your attention and focusing it to engender spirituality. When you are here now, in equipoise, concentrating on and enjoying the means, you are far better able to navigate the world. The welcome surprise is that you'll reach your destination more readily and in far better shape. You may even find that you've been tranquil and serene.

# SIX

# Family and Friends

# Visit or Call Your Parents Once a Week

*F*or most of us, no one has given more to us than our parents. Think of the equipoise required to be a good parent. Think of the unique demands your parents had placed upon them. Despite all the things that you may see wrong with your upbringing, despite your parents' shortcomings and seeming failures, most likely, they did their best. With today's critical climate urging us to perform exploratory laser surgery on every psychological blemish, it is easy to dwell on what our parents did not do, but take a moment now to think about what they did do.

Having children is about giving up, surrendering, doing without. Your parents worked hard inside and outside the house, giving of themselves to give you food, clothing, and shelter. They saw to your education and recreation. They probably spent their hard-earned money to buy you toys and books, give you lessons, and take you on vacations. They were there when you asked question after question about the world. And they gave you models of a life to live. In short, they probably raised you to the best of their ability. It's not necessary to try to reform your parents according to your ideas of what they should be like. Despite their limitations, they loved you and, above all, wanted to see you happy.

Keeping others happy is the sign of a spiritual person. When we keep others happy, we hearten them. We offer words of support and encouragement. Our native sympathy translates to our actions. We show that we truly care about them and their welfare. We happily perform our duties as friends and family members.

Spiritual people are not driven by the egotistical need to acquire first and foremost for themselves. Keeping others happy is part of seeking their own spiritual happiness. Nor does keeping others happy mean that we must go against our own natures or injure ourselves or compromise what we must do. It also does not mean that we must flatter others and build their egos. Our parents mainly want to see us, to hear from us. That makes them happy. So, visit or call your parents once a week, at least. If your parents are no longer alive, visit or call an aunt or uncle or older person who has given to you. If you live with your parents, call on a grandparent or older person who has helped parent you. By doing so selflessly to keep others happy, you are inculcating the spiritual quality of *giving*.

We are here to give to one another and help one another. Being lost in the pursuit of "for me and myself" cuts us off from our fellow living beings and our Inner Power. Highly spiritual people can keep on *giving* because they are connected to that Inner Power, that Limitless Source. They know that the more we give, the more it grows. The "it" can be anything: energy, time, money, knowledge, skill, or love. As we live lives of increased giving, we are living less in the confines of ego, and the barriers begin to disappear. Differences begin to go by the wayside, and we begin to feel that we're one. That's because we are more of the One.

Giving is performing your duty without thinking of it as a duty, without feeling hard-pressed, because the giving comes straight from your heart. True giving is done without expectation of reward or judgment that stokes your ego. When you give without thought of gain, you're giving selflessly and surrendering your ego. Being a good parent is about surrendering the ego and just giving. Remember, in our culture of self-fulfillment, where the media constantly hammers into us that we never have enough, it's easy to lose our way. We pursue what we think we want, heedlessly cutting our connections to those closest to us who have done the most for us. We need to remind ourselves and begin to understand that we are connected to all people and all living things. At least, we must start with those closest to us, giving of ourselves, helping to make those near ones happy. When we give of ourselves, we're giving our essence, which is love. By giving love, we're gaining love, for the Supreme Power, who is the Supreme Giver, is happy with us.

# The Next Time You See Your Brother or Sister, Be Kind

Growing up, many of us fought a lot with our brothers or sisters. No matter how well we got along, when one of us did or said something amiss, the other did something to get back. That hurt, so the hurt was returned in larger measure. The verbal or body blows were returned tit for tat, harder and harder, until either a parent intervened or one of us was forced to withdraw in defeat. No one could quite wound like that brother or sister. With few others do we have such a history of hurts.

What is most injurious to our spirituality? If we're committed to keeping others happy, to pleasing our Supreme Giver, the thing that is most opposed to that is injuring the feelings of others. Injuring the feelings of others is tantamount to piercing their hearts with a sword. A physical cut can heal in time, but a wound inflicted by hurtful speech may never heal. When we wound the heart of another by our words or actions, that is a great sin. To "sin" simply means to go away from God. When we hurt another person, we go away from God, because God resides in us all. The Lord dwells not only in the center of our consciousness but also in our hearts. We are all of God and from God.

Because our souls are particles of the Supreme Spirit, when we hurt another person, we are going against the Supreme Spirit and hurting ourselves as well as others, for we are all connected. In essence, we are One. *Thus, not injuring others is the paramount rule of spirituality.* The quality that precludes our hurting others is **kindheartedness**. **Kindheartedness** is what we treasure most in family, friends, classmates, colleagues, adversaries, and strangers. A kind heart, a loving heart, a soft heart would rather do anything than hurt another's feelings. In surveys asking single people what they most desire in a mate, the number one quality is kindness.

A person who is kind is gentle, considerate, and inclined to benevolent actions. A kindhearted person is also nice. It's easy to be nice to a person who's done nothing to hurt you and who is nice to you. It's a lot harder to be nice to someone whom you've fought with for years.

## ❖ Activity ❖

The next time you see your brother or sister, be kind. If you don't have a brother or sister, choose someone with whom you have a long history of closeness but with whom that closeness has also been full of barbs. Being kind means not saying anything that could possibly hurt the other person's feelings. When you know someone well, you don't even have to think about sticking that person's points of vulnerability. It's ever so easy—and in the past, it's been ever so satisfying—to say, let drop, or let fly something that barbs or nicks or cuts your target. What you're doing is nicking part of that person's heart. So, stop it. Be kind and nice.

Be genuinely nice, but don't be falsely nice. If you feel that this will be difficult, first, visualize the person and remember your relationship. Do your best to accept that person. It isn't always possible to understand why someone has acted a particular way, but appreciate that that person had a burden. He or she came into this world with weaknesses and suffered setbacks and hurts that you know nothing about. If the resentment you're harboring against that person really stands between you, you first have to practice forgiveness. You may find it necessary and helpful to establish communication about your relationship.

Communicating your actual feelings about a relationship can be difficult, but the potential rewards are great. Communicate with the intention of working things out and regaining the person as your good relation or friend. Ask for the other person's account of the events that still rankle you, with the intention of understanding why the person acted that way. Relate your experience without judgment, without trying to score points or prove that you were right or suffered most. Thus, you may remove barriers to being kind. If you've been feeling rancor toward your brother or sister, acknowledge yourself for having a kind heart and, when all is said and done, just wanting to love that person. Then, instill confidence in yourself, and act to remove the barriers, healing the hurts so that you can be kind. This will make you feel *much better*. We are all suffering, and inculcating kindheartedness works to remove suffering, not only that of those close to you but your own, too.

# Help a Friend Who Is Ill

We are all suffering in varying degrees in this life. Those who are ill are particularly suffering. If a friend of yours is ill, ask that friend what you could possibly do to help. Whether it's shopping, housework, errands, paperwork, or keeping the person company, there are any number of things that may help.

When someone accepts your help, that person is giving you a wonderful opportunity. You're not only helping that person but you also have the opportunity to grow in *compassion*. On seeing the suffering of another, you have the opportunity to feel in your heart the suffering of that person. When your heart softens and you feel ***compassion*** for that person, you become more selfless and rise closer to God, your Higher Power, which is complete compassion.

## ❖ Activity ❖

Think of a friend or an acquaintance whom you like who is ill. If you can't think of someone who is ill, one of your friends may very well be ill, but you may not know it, because you've been out of touch. In your vicinity, whom have you not seen or talked to in some time? If someone has dropped out of sight or hearing, it may be because of illness. Someone may desperately need your company or help but be too shy or overwhelmed to ask.

If you can't find someone who is ill, who in your life has been going through tough times—for example, the death of a loved one, the loss of a job, the loss of a major relationship—and may need your help? If you can't connect with a single person who needs your assistance, at which organization would you like to volunteer? If you can't think of an organization, look in the yellow pages under "Social Service Organizations."

One aspect of true community is that we respond to the needs of another within our own capabilities. Living in a community consciously, responsibly, and actively provides opportunities for growing naturally in compassion. Living compassionately in a community means that we care not only about our own advancement, materially as well as spiritually, but also about the well-being of all members, including those at the bottom. Those at the so-called bottom may be far more spiritually rich than those with whom we aspire to consort. We transcend the idea that these persons are just "filler" people, of no special advantage, because we are all part of the whole. Of course, there is no limit to how we conceive the expanse of community, only our own thinking.

Plan to make your call, and notice if any barriers come up for you, such as, "I'm just too busy to help." "No, I have too many important things going on in my life right now." "There's not much I can do to help." Or, "They probably don't want me horning in." Or perhaps you have a strong, inarticulable feeling of just not wanting to do it.

Break through your barriers and make your call with a pen and paper handy to take notes. If the person is not available, leave a message or keep calling periodically. Ask your friend or acquaintance who is ill if there's anything you could possibly do to help. If you're calling someone who has dropped out of sight, inquire politely and sincerely about how they have been. Then go on from there. Offer the person your company or assistance doing errands, and ask if there's anything else that needs to be done. Don't feel that you need to take on a heavy burden that may be too difficult to manage. Just agree to do what you know you can do. Make a specific agreement in which you will be present to help that person. Keep your agreement.

When you're helping, from your limited vantage point, appreciate that person's struggles and suffering yet also respect their privacy and boundaries. Ascertain with delicacy and care the extent to which your friend may wish to open up and talk. Don't take responsibility for solving that friend's life; just be there. Let any feelings of compassion and selflessness come naturally. Watch your feelings so that, if you feel superior or prideful, you can shush your mind and tell it that it should feel grateful for the opportunity to serve.

For, in serving by doing what you can to alleviate suffering, you are transcending boundaries and glorifying the One Power in us all. As you give your life to others, compassion grows; and as compassion grows, you become worthier to receive grace. Grace is what enables you to grow in your divinity and what helps you gain your true life.

# SEVEN

# *Inner Work*

# Spend a Day Alone

One of the spiritual advantages of being ill may be the opportunity to face being alone and to do inner work. But for many, there can be no worse fate. Many people would rather do anything than choose their own company. Why is it so terrible? You know, we really do enter this world alone and leave it alone.

Think, for a moment, about how much time you actually spend alone. Don't count time watching TV, or listening to the radio or sound system in your car or home. No matter how you feel at home with your mate, eliminate that, too. Even eliminate time you spend swept up in a fantasy or an obsessive train of thought. Just how much time do you spend alone? It could be almost none, such is your fear of being lonely.

But if you wish to develop your spirituality, it is necessary to spend time alone. This is necessary for the inner work. The actual amount of time that you are able to spend varies according to your living situation and responsibilities. But the bottom line is that you must learn to *accept and, ultimately, to enjoy your own company.*

People who actively pursue a spiritual path but who can't tolerate their own company lack the inner environment for progressing along certain key lines. Granted, on one hand, if we're serious about spirituality, we must learn to practice the virtues in whatever situation we find ourselves, and interacting with people never fails to provide particular challenges. Yet, if we are unable to enjoy our own company and spend time alone, we will lack the inner focus of attention necessary to achieve concentration and triumph over the mind. We simply must be willing to make the initial sacrifice—to find our mark, be alone, and be still.

To pursue a wholly spiritual life, rulers have given up their kingdoms and gone on pilgrimages or taken up new royal residences in forests, with birds as their only audience. That isn't necessary. An active spiritual life can be pursued along with your everyday life, right where you are. In some ways, this is even more challenging. The challenges that have been placed in your own backyard are there for a particular purpose. They're yours to surmount for the exercise you need to strengthen your spirituality. And if you're intent, you will decide to spend time alone.

## ❖ Activity ❖

Spend a day alone. If this is not possible, then make it a half-day. But make sure that no one will talk to you or interrupt your being alone. If you live with others and it isn't practical to have a space to yourself or to go somewhere overnight, then schedule a day for yourself when you take off at the first whisper of dawn and return when night is again bidding you surcease. Perhaps you can spend your day in a nature preserve. This is your day to be alone from people and with your Higher Power.

This may give you your first true taste of *solitude*. When practiced with spiritual intent, *solitude* is actually not about being alone away from people but about allowing your spiritual senses to be tuned, contacting your higher Self, and opening to your Higher Power. Your Self *craves* that. Thus, much of the real struggle into higher consciousness must be spent alone, dealing with the machinations of the lower mind, overcoming negative thoughts, leaning inward with the soul, communing with the Higher Power.

Solitude enables you to open to the divine goodness and powers that are ever-present. Solitude presents an opportunity to encounter and become aware of your true Self, not the false self that you plaster on as the situation requires. And please remember, you are not your thoughts. You are much more. You are a wonder that elicits awe. The practice of solitude provides an opportunity to contact that wonder. The challenge is to come to know that solitude is a gift, a gift you give your Self.

As you begin your period of solitude, prepare for it with the attitude that you are giving a precious gift to your Self. See this as a much deserved time to relax and feel the value of your human life. Know that whatever comes up, you have the power and capabilities to collect yourself, calm yourself, and center yourself. You understand your mind more than before and you are using your time alone to better learn when it is friend or foe.

During your day alone, you may wish to practice some of the activities and exercises included in this book and other books. You will not lose yourself in entertainments, and any time spent reading or listening will be utilized as a springboard to delve deeper into your retreat. For your time alone is a spiritual retreat, a God-given chance to begin to return to who you are, to who you are meant to be. Actually, to who you have always been. You possess the creative imagination and the resources to make this a time of great value and richness. Practicing solitude, you can come closer to appreciating all that you have and may have.

# Reframe a Recurring Negative Thought

You may have looked forward to your day of solitude as a day of stillness and richness and instead found that you slid into a funk of discombobulation. You may have endeavored to meditate but found that your mind was out of control, seething with scenes of confrontation, wallowing in fantasies of suffering and self-pity, or imagining character assassinations from every quarter. That may be why you resist solitude; it just brings up too much. You prefer not to be assailed by your mind unleashed. Yet, stuffing your yapping mad dog of a mind in a hamper doesn't do it. You can still hear it. And sooner than later, it will jump out at you.

The one thing that carries people furthest from their spiritual center is negative thoughts. Negative thoughts are unloving thoughts rooted in the downward passions of anger, ego, attachment, greed, and lust. They're false thoughts that are divorced from clear reality. We're not talking about pleasant fantasies and daydreams over which you have control but mental scenes and confrontations that are riding on your back, yapping in your ear. And try as you might, you can't shake them. Negative thoughts are also just plain conversations and scenes, unresolved from the past or anticipated for the future, that keep playing over and over again in your mind. And try as you may, you can't change the tune. You're a captive audience to this broken record.

Wake up, the enemy is your lower mind. You allow it to run roughshod over you, ordering your every emotion and motion. You allow it to usurp your true identity and purpose and freedom, robbing you of your God-given birthright. But its power is so great and its tricks so relentlessly nefarious that the more you resist it, the stronger it apparently becomes. Even powerful repetition of a mantra or affirmation can have no effect when your mind is on a binge.

Now, as you become more aware of your mind's tendency to rule you with negative thoughts and scenes, don't go into a reaction mode and judge them. They're merely stuck, downward energy that await resolution. And please, don't judge yourself. You are where you are. Always imbibe self-love. Furthermore, this doesn't mean that you *identify* with your thoughts, even though that's what most people do. What you can do is use your growing awareness to focus your spiritual power and reclaim the bliss that your lower mind destroys or prevents you from having.

Don't judge your mind. It is just doing its job. And you can learn to do yours. Do you want to go through life being a victim of thoughts that can be so out of control and poisonous that you may as well be bitten by a rabid dog? Well, what can you do? The solution is to de-fang it while you give it a higher pleasure. The higher pleasure comes from attending to your spiritual practices with single-minded desire and intention. The de-fanging is draining the negative energy from your mind and re-framing your thoughts so that they're rooted in detached, objective reality.

Perhaps you're one of the lucky few who is unblemished by negative thoughts. You own your energy as well as your mind. However, the mind is so smart and sly that you may forget that you've had negative sessions. When you're not being plagued by negative thoughts, they have a tendency to get buried and forgotten. This doesn't mean that something won't set them off. You still have stuck negative energy with certain people. Anything can set it off, and then once again, you are harassed. When the mind is between sessions, it's easy to forget how it has commandeered you.

Try this exercise to get in touch with the effect of negative thoughts on your spirituality. Feel free to tape yourself reading this exercise and then play it back for yourself.

## ❖ Exercise ❖

Take a slow, deep breath, release it gently, and close your eyes. Think of a person about whom or a situation about which you recently had recurring mental conversations or negative thoughts. Go back to a time when you recently had a negative thought about a person or situation, and notice how you were feeling. . . . What were they saying and what were you saying in your mind? What wasn't happening and what wasn't being said? Notice how you felt in your body when that scene was playing in your mind. . . . Notice how much power that kind of thinking has on the way that you feel about yourself.

Continue, and when you're having those thoughts, notice how you really feel. . . . Notice how far they take you away from your spiritual grounding or center. Well, you have the power to reclaim your spiritual center. Imagine the person with whom you were having a scene, and picture that person outside your dwelling. Now, place the person in a giant rubber balloon. That person may try to pester you or shout, but you can choose not to hear them. They can try to say things that disturb you, but they can't affect you. In fact, you can separate from that person. You can free the energy that is stuck between you.

Keeping the person in the balloon, name five things that are *neutral* and different about the two of you, things that sizzle with neither a positive nor negative charge for you. For instance, "I was born in March and he was born in July. I own a white car and he owns a black truck. I own a Honda and he owns a Ford. My first name has seven letters and his has six letters. I have curly hair and he has straight hair." These five things can be anything as long as you don't have a charge on them.

Continue to picture the person in a balloon, tethered outdoors. Now, speaking from your heart and from your center of power, tell the person what you need to say. Perhaps you can't be a certain way that that person wants you to be. Or, perhaps the person hasn't supported you or communicated with you, or did something that really hurt you. Perhaps the person failed to act in a way that you felt was right and appropriate. Say whatever you need to. If you're angry with the person, kick or hit the balloon. It won't hurt the occupant.

Now, fill the balloon with helium, release the rope, and see it rise quickly into the sky. Send it off, far away, over a body of water, far enough so that you feel perfectly safe. Once your mind's eye sees that it's over the safe destination—a lake or somewhere over the ocean—see it either disappear, pop, or explode loudly with all its pieces falling gently to the water. This won't hurt the balloon's occupant; it just releases the stuck energy between the two of you. Repeat this as long as you're feeling riled by the person, using the visual imagery that you feel is most effective.

When you feel that you're finally reaching a place of neutrality, free energy, and peace, create still another balloon, put the person inside, and recall the negative thoughts you've been having. . . . Then objectively tell the truth about the situation to defuse your negative feelings, and you will reframe your negative thoughts into something positive. Here's an example.

Perhaps your boyfriend or someone else has been driving you crazy, and you feel really bad about him *and* your thoughts because, in addition to the unrelenting mental scenes you've been suffering, you're also thinking, "You creep. . ." or "You pig!" A way to reframe this is to think, "I notice that ＿＿＿＿＿＿＿＿＿＿ (fill in the person's name) has brought up some feelings within me because of the way that he talked to me. And I notice that when I acknowledge it in this way, it defuses the negative feelings I have. When it feels like he is pulling on me, I know it's because he wants something. He's being demanding because he's feeling needy. And, for now, he can't help it. That's his way. And I don't need his approval nor do I need to do what he wants, because I accept and love myself. Because of this, I take responsibility for meeting my needs first."

This is an example of a positive reframe. The actual details of your situation are for you to name. Now, return to your negative thoughts, the scenes that keep playing in your mind, and take a moment to *shift* and *reframe* those negative thoughts into something positive and knowing about that person. With compassion, truth, and understanding, reframe the negative thoughts into something positive and objective. . . .

Notice how much closer you feel to your spiritual roots and your own center. . . . Part of this change may be deciding to maturely take responsibility and resolving to take action, such as communicating with the person to express your needs and boundaries. When you do that, notice how you feel less victimized by your mind and how much more relaxed, peaceful, centered, and in touch with your spiritual core you feel.

Now, please open your eyes and bring your attention back into the room. Take a deep breath and stretch, if you wish. Feel free to write about your experience.

Practicing this process helps you develop the faculty of *positive thinking*. *Positive thinking* includes clear, objective, mature, detached thinking and is a crucial faculty that you must develop if you are ever to begin becoming master of your mind.

Many people don't realize that they're at the mercy of their minds. They have no idea how often, during the day, they step onto a roller-coaster ride that takes them through a house of horrors at breakneck speed. The coaster careens and caroms past frights that seize their mental states. Not until some new outer urgency demands their attention do they pass out of that house of horrors and get off the ride, dizzy and queasy. They never realize that they, in fact, allowed those inner scenes to commandeer their reality and inner state.

Instead of getting on a ride that leaves you weak-kneed and wobbly, wouldn't you like to lay your own tracks and move along them at your own speed, passing by sights and sounds of your own choosing? Just because you're having these so-called negative thoughts, you don't have to let them be your reality. Don't judge them. See them as stuck energy that you can unstick. See this as an opportunity to learn about your mind and how you can outsmart it to practice autonomy and other strengths. You can learn to train your mind and turn it into your friend. Clear, positive thinking can actually open fabulous new areas to you.

Often, persistent negative thoughts are a sign that you have issues to work out and resolve with the person involved. If this is the case, why not contact that person to say that you'd like to discuss the problem in an open, nonpressured setting? Then get together and allow each of you to communicate what is true for you about the situation. The positive aspect of those negative thoughts may be an opportunity to practice acceptance and forgiveness.

If you have persistent, obsessive negative thoughts, you may wish to consider working with a therapist or a healer. But ultimately, you must do the work. You are the one who must notice that you've left your spiritual center, that place of calm and centeredness and purpose. You are the one who has your mind. You are the one who must observe its patterns and learn to reprogram it. And you are the one who can change its switch tracks so that, instead of going on a ride that assails you, you can climb safely into new country. Until you learn to reframe negative thoughts, you will continue to miss out on much.

# Make an Accounting of Everything You Have

Do you ever feel that, for all your abilities and talents and good efforts, you've received the short end of the stick? Do you mainly concentrate on what is missing in your life? In our culture of acquisitiveness and perfectionism, it is easier to see the half-empty glass that's lacking water, while ignoring the half-full glass.

We tend to go through life focusing on what we want—a higher-paying job, a new car, a primary relationship, a trip to Europe, better children or parents, winning the lottery. . . . The list goes on and on.

## ❖ Activity ❖

Sit down without interruption for 15 minutes or so, and make an accounting of everything you have. Include everything, even though it may be temporary, even though it all must be given up when you leave this life. Start with things like five senses that work, legs and arms that work, enough clothes, money to buy food, a home to live in, parents who did their best to raise you, a child who is a good person, a way to make money, and people who like you and care for you. Keep writing down things as fast as you can. Don't think about it. Be as specific and as general as you can. Don't discount what comes up. However insignificant it seems, write it down. You might be paralyzed from the waist down; you might be deaf. Never mind. Make the rest of your list that much longer.

When you have completed your list, read it over. Add to it. Fold your list so that it can neatly fit into a pocket. If you're not wearing clothing with a convenient pocket, change into something that has a good-size pocket. Insert your list into a pocket of your clothing and carry it with you during the day. From time to time, especially when you sense a constriction, a want, take out your list, read it, and revel in it.

With this process, the joyful flower of *gratitude* may bloom in your heart. When awareness of everything you have dawns in you, how do you feel? Don't you have an extraordinary abundance to be thankful for? *Gratitude* is being thankful, grateful for what you have. With gratitude firmly rooted in your heart, you are humble and open and receptive and inducing your Benefactor to shower you with more gifts, physical and spiritual. And it's more than gifts! A grateful heart is a grace-full heart. A grace-full heart is one that is open, alive, and growing toward communion with its Benefactor.

If you insist on taking credit for everything you have—"I did it my way!"—go ahead. But try to observe what happens when you close yourself down from your Higher Power. Eventually, you may wish to be back as a junior-junior-junior partner in all this.

Do you realize that you have been given *exactly* what you need just so that you may proceed with the spiritual lessons and growth that you, you alone, need to master? Yes, life can be absolutely daunting, but you can have gratitude when you realize that you have just what you need. Gratitude is the virtue that shifts our energy in order to facilitate our great growth to the next levels. *Without the hankering* after what we don't have, we allow ourselves to receive from God just what we need. Then we have and use just what we need to, so that we're prepared for greater gifts and gains inside.

# EIGHT

# Spirituality without Judgment

# Welcome Red Lights

When you're trying to get somewhere, red lights can be really aggravating. You're making good progress, but then you're stopped. Often, you could have made it through, but for the slow driver who got in the way.

Jockeying for position on the freeway, drivers have been shot. Such is the world we live in, where cutting in place to gain a five-second advantage can trigger murder. But that person who cut you off might be rushing to the hospital to see his dying father; and that slow driver who's going nowhere near the speed limit might be in a daze because she just lost her mother. Or, that may be the way they usually drive. Even if you actually found out why those drivers were behaving so miserably, minutes later, very late for an appointment, you could find yourself at the rear of a five-mile backup. You'd be too far back to get out, find the errant drivers, and demand an explanation. For some reason, people refuse to behave perfectly in accordance with your master plan.

Until everyone does follow your plan and nothing happens to mar your beatitude, please realize what effect getting upset has on you. You might want to shoot the driver who cuts you off. You might want to slam into the car that is crawling in front of you. You might be unbelievably late, only to be stopped by a red light and sit there seething, willing it to change. What are you giving up? How far have you traveled from your spiritual center? Since you're becoming an astute observer, determine what effect anger, anxiety, impatience, and frustration have on you.

We call these *negative* emotions because they take us away from our spiritual center and split us off from our Self. If, going through the traffic of life, we allow ourselves to become angry, anxious, impatient, or frustrated, we are indulging the most basic of judgments. The judgment is that others are not behaving the way we think they should. But the world is filled with bad drivers. If you feel a strong commitment toward reforming those who are speed-challenged, consider becoming a highway patrol officer or judge.

But be prepared to discover that these errant souls consider themselves splendid drivers.

The judgment that you are right can lead to all kinds of problems, like high blood pressure, moving violations, mangled steel, and broken necks. Don't allow the slightest provocation of imperfection to make you regress to an infantile state, in effect causing a dark caul to cover your face, masking your spiritual sight. Instead, use this as an opportunity to engage in inner work and to imbibe spirituality without judgment. Please start with this.

### ❖ Activity ❖

When you come to a red light, take a deep breath and welcome it. Welcome the red light as an opportunity to stop, come to the present, and check your attention. Where has it been? How many miles ahead of you has it been? Now, identify the red light as a signal to practice *patience*. *Patience* is an integral component of the character needed for spiritual progress.

Practicing patience is an opportunity to let go and let God, and to transmute negative emotions into positive virtues. With patience, you are relaxed and centered; you have energy and attention that you can readily draw on; and you can proceed with the assurance that things are in their rightful place, even though you may not necessarily like them. Patience is absolutely essential if you wish to keep treading your spiritual path. As you pass through the initial inspiration and fervor of pursuing your spirituality and finally face the everyday dryness, boredom, and lack of quick results, patience is an essential tool in your toolbox of qualities. Patience will keep you centered, surrendered, detached, and content to just continue with the assurance that, "Yes, everything in its good time."

True spirituality is about losing the ego and letting your consciousness expand into your Higher Power. There is a higher Will operating most efficiently in this world, although most of us are not privy to it. Remember that when we make judgments that things are not happening the way *we think* they should, this is the height of arrogance. This is acting as though our way is superior to the Higher Power's. We're acting as though we know better. But do we actually know the cause and effect of everything happening around us? While we may share in creative power, until we have merged our consciousness in the Creator, we are in absolutely no position to judge when and how things happen.

A light changing to red as you're charging along is but the most minor thing over which you may habitually lose your patience. If you can't maintain your patience over something so inconsequential, which actually is an opportunity to recenter yourself, how will you steep yourself in patience when you've been struggling for years to see inner spiritual light, without apparent progress, and you are consumed by your judgments, just wanting to toss in the towel?

The key to mastering everyday spirituality is first mastering the baby steps. Study and learn how spirituality affects, offers opportunities in, and challenges every aspect of your everyday life. Then set out gently on your path to inculcate the spiritual virtues step by step, light by light.

# For a Week, Eliminate Expectations and Concentrate on What Is at Task

For all we know, we could wait at a red light and it might never change. That's happened before. Or, it could start flashing amber. Or, it could change to blue. Or, stranger things could happen. When we have set ideas of how things should manifest, of how things will happen to us, we're limiting the possibilities of luck, chance connections, grace, and miracles. When we're set on something, and it has to happen that way, we're closing the door to wonderful surprises. When a hand keeps grasping after something, it's not open, waiting to receive.

We have expectations about everything in life. We expect that something will come in the mail, that we're going to have a fantastic vacation, that a stock will rise 40 percent by January, that the new people in our lives are going to do wonderful things for us, that our children will succeed in life. By projecting these expectations, we're attempting to order reality. Not only are we proclaiming how reality should be but also we're deciding that we know what is best for us.

This is the height of egotism. Ego or I-ness cuts us off from our Source and separates us from our Higher Power. The force of ego is about making its own mountain for all the world to see, and standing tall at its summit. The force of love is about serving our Higher Power, glorifying that divine connection, and letting our ego slip away while we flow freely in the stream of life, striving to realize the heart-felt goals that express our highest, best Self.

As our spirituality develops and we live more in higher consciousness, we exist more fully in the present. Existing in present time, we're less aware of ourselves and time, flowing in that higher consciousness, so that time begins to feel almost elastic and almost nonexistent. That elasticity is the beginning of eternity. Beginning to enter into eternity is not possible unless the ego is surrendered. When we're attached to our expectations—in effect, demanding that events unfold according to *our will*—we are energizing our ego and telling our Higher Power that we know best.

Relinquishing expectations is not being passive. It's the opposite; it's freeing ourselves to concentrate on the task at hand and to flow with what is truly so. What is so is the reality occurring now, which we need to recognize and respond to.

## ❖ Exercise ❖

For a week, eliminate expectations to concentrate on what is at task. This exercise will require much alertness. You really have to watch your mind. Each time you're aware of an expectation—whether it be that you will receive a phone call from a particular person or that a check will come in the mail or that you'll be crazy about the movie you're going to see—write it down on a scrap of paper and throw it away. Once you throw it away, redirect your attention to the task at hand and concentrate on it. Keep doing this. You really want to tire out your desiring, expectant mind.

You also need to discriminate between expectation and intuition. Expectation is when you decide how something should happen. Intuition is simply a knowing. It comes unbidden. It is effortless and usually comes just when you need to know. An expectation is more a desire that hardens into a hope that petrifies into an expectation. It's an attachment of the mind that feels like blocked energy. Something has to happen your way. Your mind is attempting to order future reality. With expectation, you're set up for disappointment; whereas, with intuition, out of nowhere, you notice a breeze. It feels right, and you just know.

Eliminating expectations does not at all mean that you stop your good intentions. You can form the intention and let go of it, letting your Higher Power work out the details in your best interest. That is *humility*. A humble person can have potent intention but relinquish nitty-gritty expectations about the how and when. In *humility*, you surrender to your Higher Power and want your attention free to be with that Higher Love.

The greater the immersion in that Higher Love, the less strident the ego's demands. Operating from ego or pride is treating yourself as though you are the beginning and end of the world. All that matters is the immediate satisfaction of your sensual appetites and the dictates of your mind. But lasting satisfaction never comes. The nonhumble ego always wants more money, more possessions, more pleasure, more adulation, more status, more luxury, more ease, more power. The stories of those who set themselves up as modern-day potentates so that they can rule and expand their fiefdoms makes great fodder for the tabloids and the slick monthlies. This is mainly because these egos always fall, and many of us secretly enjoy their falls. Why? Because, inside, we know that the right way is in humility.

Eliminating expectations is but one small feature of inculcating humility. Reams could be written about humility, the most beautiful of virtues and the most difficult to ultimately receive. For ultimately, humility is not grabbed, as if you are a corporate raider intent on amassing the most virtuous spiritual portfolio. It's a very slow, natural process. Unaware of itself, humility proceeds as the attention is intent on devotion, so intent that your yearning for your Higher Power burns away the shrill, scratchy static of your ego. And after your ceaseless efforts have left you feeling stripped bare of all that you are and have, knowing that, in fact, on your own, you are nothing, then with grace, unaware, you are transmuted a little more in humility.

# Clean Your Home Humbly and Lovingly

Consider two housecleaners. The first shows up late, complains about low pay, indignantly informs you that doing windows is not in the job description, breaks a vase and throws it away without telling you, tracks in dirt while giving the house a cursory cleaning, and makes long-distance calls after eating your box of chocolates. The second housecleaner shows up on time, charges you a reasonable rate, gladly does windows, cleans things that you are too meek to ask about but are thrilled to have cleaned, and is cheerful, conscientious, and happily does all that you bid. Which housecleaner would you prefer?

When you houseclean, you are removing dirt from an abode. That is humble work. A housecleaner who does the job well performs the wonderful service of bringing cleanliness and order to the environment of the employer. Along with providing cleanliness and order, a housecleaner supports the employer's moving forward in life. Finally, an extra-special housecleaner adds a higher feeling to that environment, which helps the resident feel good and content to be there.

## ❖ Activity ❖

Clean your home humbly and lovingly. If you are physically unable to clean your entire home, then clean a portion of it, like a table. Work hard, cheerfully, conscientiously, and without thought of reward. Assume that your employer is the Big Giver who is putting your wages in trust, to be given to you only when you are sufficiently clean to enjoy them in humility.

As you clean, look sharply for things that you or the regular housecleaner usually miss. Also, imagine what your house would be like if you continued living in it while dust, dirt, and disorder kept building for 3 weeks, 6 weeks, 12 weeks, and 24 weeks. Think about what your house would be like if dirt accumulated for 1 year, 2 years, 4 years, and 16 years. Finally, imagine your home if you continued living in it uncleaned for 64 years.

Now, think of the days of your life when you did nothing to stop your negative thoughts, hurtful speech, and harmful actions; when you did nothing to induce positive thoughts, healing speech, and helpful actions. Always remember, *you* are the temple of your Higher Power. Your temple is holy and wonderfully precious. But if you don't clean your vessel regularly, what dirt accumulates? If you are not regularly practicing or inculcating a spiritual quality, what downward tendencies will accumulate?

Now, continuing to clean, clean *lovingly*. You're not just removing dust and dirt, you are imbuing every surface, the whole atmosphere, with love so that everything sparkles with more than cleanliness. The floor, the tables, and the objects can all shimmer with love.

So, what is the point of all this? What is the benefit? If you don't do the exercise properly, you'll probably receive no benefit. And that's the rub. With expectations, with demands for quid pro quo for your spiritual work, you may get paid eventually, but how ready will your Giver be? A person who is working on the spiritual path, who is dedicated and humble and is doing it just out of love for the Higher Power, is doing it just to please God. Such a person will most surely evoke *grace*.

If we perform our spiritual work with a good attitude, like a housecleaner who works quietly, humbly, and lovingly instead of carelessly and feeling like put-upon royalty, we become receptive to

***grace***. Grace is simply whatever brings us closer to God. We can think of grace as a constant showering of manna from heaven. Grace is food for the soul. It's what enables us to come even closer to and ever more into God.

We can't force God, bribe God, nor even cajole God to give us that grace. It's not in our power. We can only do our best to keep our cups right side up so that we can catch the grace being showered on us. Turning our cups right side up is reading spiritual literature, imbibing virtues like forgiveness, controlling tendencies like greed, and remembering our Higher Power.

Doing all these things and more is making an ***effort***. With that grace, we make an ***effort***. Grace and effort are the two wings of the mystical bird that fly you toward your Beloved. Allow Beloved to mean whatever feels right for you: your Higher Power, Jesus Christ, a Saint or Master. Without grace, you cannot even think of your Beloved nor pray nor make the slightest effort. Yet, every true and humble effort evokes grace. The process is a circle—actually, one wondrous upward spiral. As your spiritual path continues to come more closely into focus, your whole vast undertaking can be distilled into this: Make an effort and look for grace.

Making an effort means doing your very best to imbibe the virtues every step of the way. It means practicing your spiritual practice with discernment, discipline, and discrimination. Making an effort means engaging in a constant struggle with your lower mind, that great power that uses every trick to lead you away from your hard-won progress.

Laziness and inertia are perhaps the greatest enemies of the spiritual practitioner. It's so easy and feels so comfortable to become a couch potato that you don't even realize when you sprout roots. You better act before your roots pierce the cushions. Yes, it takes great effort and intention to uproot yourself from your customary patterns. The mind is pleasure-loving and wants easy rewards. Yet remember, through effort and discipline, you can win that inner bliss that is so superior that, once you get a true taste, your former pleasures taste like dirt.

But you have to make the effort to wake yourself. And never despair, grace is always there. You just need to look for it. Looking for grace means to be attentive, alert, and present while you are making an effort, using your God-given perceptions to know that grace is being showered on you. It's letting that grace feed your soul and spur you on to greater efforts. Looking for grace means a commitment of such completeness that making an effort is giving your *all*, surrendering yourself, and transcending all judgments, so that, when the moment comes, you'll be receptive . . . and you'll catch the grace and soar.

# Squash a Bug

If only grace were readily caught. More often than not, your attention gets diverted. There is so very much to bug you.

What is your least favorite pesky bug? Is it a fly? A mosquito? A cockroach? A bumblebee? Does it land on you? Fly around your face? Threaten to hurt you? Simply revolt you by its existence? In all cases, it distracts you from whatever you're trying to do. It's a damned nuisance, a pest. Something you can be tempted to squash. If you squash one mosquito, two more may land on your head. You may be unaware of them until they've sucked out some blood. The number of bugs is unlimited. For every one you kill, several can take its place.

While you may feel fully justified in killing as many bugs as you can, please remember that they're living creatures, too. Rather than waging war against every pesky bug you hear, it's probably more effective to wear insect repellent when you're outdoors and to keep your doors shut and your home clean. In other words, if you take precautions and adjust to the situation, you can concentrate on what you're doing, rather than having your peace destroyed.

Some people in our lives are impossible pests. They're usually those closest to us, and they continually do things that make us want to swat them. In time, we view them, or at least their behavior, as a major irritant. Even when they're not doing the irritating thing, we think of how they drive us crazy. But what is really bugging us, their seemingly obnoxious behavior or our judgment of them?

### ❖ Exercise ❖

Close your eyes and settle on the one person and the one thing that person does that bug you the most. Maybe it's a noise that your partner makes, a family member's failure to clean up or to respect your boundaries, or a co-worker's failure to perform a certain job the way that you think it should be done. If you've settled on someone who has actually hurt your feelings, save that person for chapter 31, Forgive Someone Who's Hurt You, and choose another person whose behavior just really bugs you. What does that person do that bugs you?

Notice what effect that person's behavior has on you. Does this person's behavior directly affect your feelings or your bodily sensations? These observations may be like, "When so-and-so does such-and-such, I notice that I feel anxious and my stomach feels like it's constricting."

Now, notice what opinions or judgments you make as a result of the person's behavior and the way that it affects your feelings and bodily sensations. This type of judgment is a statement about the other person such as, "When so-and-so does such-and-such, they're really being a creep." Easily, the judgment becomes, "So-and-so is a total jerk." Mentally make those judgments, and notice how your feelings and body are affected. Perhaps you are feeling riled. Actually, really angry. Perhaps you are feeling nerve-racked or invaded or rejected. When making such judgments, notice where you are in relation to your spiritual center. Do you experience calmness, centeredness, or affection?

Recall the history of that person's behavior and your reactions to it. Feel the energy that has developed around the issue. As this issue has continued, have your judgments become more strident; have your reactions become more intense, more congealed? Has a charge built up around this issue? Visualize this issue in any way you can. What does it look like? Now visualize your body in relation to this issue. What does your body's reaction to the person's behavior look like? Are parts tight, scrunched up, red, throbbing? In your mind's eye, can you see how this affects your body? Do you really want to carry this with you?

Consider this. With all the good work you have done thus far, can you allow that person's process of life and seeming shortcomings and feel mercy for what the person is going through?

You may not be able to change the other person, but you can change yourself. You can decide to take the necessary steps to promote your healthy process of life as well as release the judgments of that person that keep your mind buzzing in that negative relationship.

Think of the judgments you're constantly making about that person as pesky bugs that keep flying around your head, diverting you from your true work. It is much easier to give your attention to something you don't like when your mind is making judgment after righteous judgment. It's better to squash the judgment that's buzzing in your head and to concentrate on improving yourself. By neutralizing and releasing judgments and allowing the other person the process of life, you will be practicing *acceptance*. *Acceptance* is to allow, experience, receive, tolerate, or endure *without judgment*.

Acceptance is the foundation of spirituality without judgment. Our minds are terribly fond of making judgments and would just as soon dwell all day in that fascinating hornet's nest. Develop the awareness to notice when judgments are buzzing through your head.

## ❖ Continuing Exercise ❖

Let the judgments that have been buzzing through your head form into your least favorite bug. When the person's behavior really gets to you, which kind of bug feels as though it's on your head or in your clothing? Visualize this bug being as large as your judgments. Perhaps it's one foot long. Perhaps it's six feet long. In your mind's eye, place this bug on a blank screen in front of you. This bug may be monstrous. This particular bug may be the prime candidate for the lead in a cheap sci-fi thriller. But it can't touch you, nor can it affect you adversely. Now, recalling the exercise in chapter 23, you're going to do a somewhat different version of a positive reframe.

First, find something that you feel is genuinely good about the person. For instance, "So-and-so is a vivacious person and likes to engage with people." Keep repeating this, and as you do so, an interesting thing will happen on the screen. The bug will grow smaller and smaller as your affirmation of the positive aspect of the person gives rise to a scene of that positive behavior on the screen. As the scene of that good behavior grows larger, notice the sounds, actions, smells, and colors of that scene. What aliveness does the person possess in the scene?

Repeat the following to yourself, and feel free to modify it to suit your needs. "I notice that so-and-so's behavior has brought up some feelings and judgments in me. When I acknowledge it in this way, my negative charge on that behavior is defused, and I can appreciate good aspects of this person's behavior." Now, repeat: "So-and-so, I accept you for who you are and what you do." Keep repeating it. Breathe deeply. Notice the bug. How small is it now? You can decide to co-exist with this bug of your judgments, or you can squash it. If the latter, in your mind's eye now, squash the bug.

Later, if you find yourself indulging your judgments, dwelling on how this or another person bugs you or why that person is getting away with something or why another person is getting recognition, ask yourself, "Do I want my judgments, or do I want spiritual growth? Am I willing to work to discipline my mind and imbibe acceptance so that I am free to enjoy a higher, more subtle pleasure?" If you answer this last question in the affirmative, you may wish to practice the above exercise again, tailoring it to the situation.

Accepting someone does not mean you have to be a doormat. You also need to take appropriate steps to ensure that *your process of life* proceeds healthfully, supported by the spiritual virtues. It's a fine balance. If your peace is being destroyed, if your mental health is being compromised, then you need to freshly take responsibility to take care of yourself. Ask your Higher Power for guidance on how you can establish healthy boundaries with the person who bugs you that satisfy both of your needs and duties and growth. You can establish boundaries or guidelines with the other person and still accept them.

Being in a relationship does not mean that you have to let yourself be dragged down. You are responsible for proceeding with your life. You have the power to communicate your needs and to establish healthy boundaries. You can describe your needs without making the other person wrong. You can communicate lovingly and forthrightly. You can discover and implement a solution that is fair and that supports your needs as well as your duties. Remember to start with true acceptance.

Acceptance confers great freedom. It's a recognition of reality, and once you've achieved that grounding, it's moving forward. Embrace acceptance as another mode of love in action, one that releases your negative attachment to people and frees you to progress in even more challenging virtues that foster spirituality without judgment.

# Give Up Something You Don't Like

*I*s there some aspect of your life that you don't like, that frustrates you, that you wish weren't so? If so, give it up. Just give it up.

No matter how different you feel that condition in your life should be, just give it up. For instance, if you're single and dissatisfied about it because you want to be in a primary relationship, give up your unhappiness about not being in a relationship. Don't force yourself to give up the desire to be in a relationship; rather, give up your frustration and lack of acceptance.

When you give up those feelings, you're no

longer railing against your current state. Realize how you've allowed your mind to drag you away from your spiritual center. Do you really wish to hitch your happiness to an external condition? Do you really wish to identify with a mind that goes wild and starts bucking, no matter what the terrain? By not surrendering to the condition of being single, you've allowed yourself to be unhappy. Yet people who are coupled just as readily allow themselves to be unhappy in relationships that could be ideal.

When you're railing against something, you're stuck on something that is not working. By clinging to what you don't have *now*, you're attached to it; you're operating with egotism. There's no space or energy around the issue. You're suffocating it with judgments. Your position is that *you* know what is best for you. When you insist that you must have something, according to what you think is best, but then you don't have it, you become divided. You split off from part of your spiritual center. And then you're unhappy. When you assert that you know what is best, you're putting your will above that of your Higher, All-Knowing Power. If you truly accept God, do you actually wish to do this?

## ❖ Affirmation ❖

Invent an effective affirmation for your issue that deals with the emotions of not liking that particular aspect of your life. In the example of wanting to be in a primary relationship, an affirmation could be, "I can be perfectly happy right now, even without a primary relationship."

If your truth remains that you still wish to be in the right relationship, why not affirm that you're doing those very things that will prepare you for and attract your primary relationship? Don't repeat, "I want a relationship. Why can't I have a relationship?" pestering for it, emphasizing your lack, and remaining oblivious to the counterproductive effect of doing so. Instead, further your goal by repeating, "I easily do those things and am being those ways that will attract the best relationship for me." Rather than re-energizing lack, this shifts your energy and aligns you with the positive reality that you wish to energize.

By doing this, you are concentrating constructively, in three steps, to manifest something that your Self identifies with, but which hasn't yet come into your reality. The first step is knowing the core energy of what you wish to be true, without inner or external judgment. In the example, that energy is a strong connection with a kindred soul, which is mutually supportive, loving, and conducive to advancement in all areas of life. This energizes desire and intention.

The second step is knowing the form that you want your goal to take. In the example, that form is a monogamous primary relationship. Visualize all of its qualities. This is focusing your attention and watching it grow.

By visualizing the relationship in all its wonderful qualities, you're further drawing the relationship to you. What's more, you're inducing happiness. Instead of constantly judging your state negatively, which just reinforces your unhappiness and the state you'd prefer to not be in, you are repeatedly visualizing the qualities that you desire to have in your life. Instead of filling your illusory time with the unhappiness of not having, you are surrendering to the moment, which is all you really have, and making it be the best that you can. Thus, this is the third step: surrendering in a way that doesn't interfere with guidance. By surrendering in a way that allows you to be calm, sure, neutral, and harmonious, you are being *open* to guidance to do those things and be those ways that further your growth into the person you must be to surely attract the right partner to you.

### ❖ Affirmation ❖

Invent another effective affirmation for your issue that will mobilize you to attract the reality you are seeking and start you on this three-step process. It could begin, "I easily do those things and am being those ways that. . . . " This also helps to trick the mind in a way that will bring success. The mind likes repetition in its reality.

By not judging, but by accepting and doing with single-mindedness, you're not giving up on your goal. What you're doing is giving up your insistence that your goal be manifested in the way you want it to be. You are accepting reality and embracing truth. At the same time, you are working in accordance with the reality to best facilitate the realization of your goal. You continue working toward the goal, but you let go of the results because you realize that you're not in charge of the results. God is. You are concentrating on *your* work, your own effort. If something isn't happening the way that *you* want it to, so what? By trying to impose your exact idea of how something should turn out, you're most likely ensuring that it won't turn out at all. Remember, your work is the effort.

By devoting ourselves to this spiritual process, we will gain our true prize, **surrender**. **Surrender** is a deep form of acceptance that means flowing with the Will of the Higher Power. As long as we have egotism and are not in full communion with the Supreme Spirit, we can't live in complete surrender. But we can develop surrender as our consciousness blooms in love of our Higher Power. We can definitely make that effort.

*Acceptance* applies more to outer conditions that we need to experience and allow without judgment, while *surrender* connotes a deeper flowing or merging with Divine Will. Surrender is an inner posture, an alignment that takes us deeper into the mystical mystery of humility and love. It's a giving up to God and a trusting in the unfolding process of our soul's growth that results in purification of our hearts.

Perhaps you've wondered why someone (an actor is a good example) may work toward a goal for most of a lifetime but not achieve outward success, while another person with the same or even less talent can be discovered and become an overnight sensation and then a major star. Most of us don't yet have the spiritual insight to actually know the whys and wherefores of how things happen the way that they do. That is why, if we're intent on practicing spirituality without judgment, we must *give it up to God*.

❖   Exercise   ❖

Please read through this paragraph, then enact it in your mind's eye. Settle on something you want that is your heart's desire but that you don't have, something you are aching for. It could be having a primary relationship, owning your own business, not being a smoker or drug user, traveling to a place you've always dreamed about, or being genuinely cheerful or giving. Visualize what reaching that goal would be like — the scenes, smells, sights, even the emotions. Now, give that up mentally. Give that desire to God. Repeat mentally and out loud, "I give this to God." See yourself hand the thing that's bothering you to God. And see loving arms take it away.

## ❖ Continuing Exercise ❖

Read through this paragraph, then close your eyes and visualize it as well as you can. Return to the situation that's been really rankling you because it is not the way that you want it to be. Feel the desire of really wanting it to be the way that you want it. Feel the frustration. Commend yourself for the good efforts you've made toward righting it or achieving that goal.

Now, in your mind's eye, put everything—the desire, the unrealized pictures, the efforts, the frustrations, the defeats, whatever you've visualized—into a large box. Take a beautiful piece of wrapping paper and wrap up the box. Put a bow on it. No matter how big that box, you have the strength to lift it, so give it to your Higher Power. That Higher Power takes it lovingly, and you are at peace, and glowing with power and resolve to go forward.

Giving begets receiving. Great spiritual focus resides in giving. When you truly give up something, when you *surrender*, you are freed. You are freed from stuck energy, from negative thoughts, and from retarding mental patterns. You are freed to come more fully into your true life, progressing in self-realization and creatively discerning, free of judgments, your own spirituality.

# Look at Something You Don't Like as Being for Your Spiritual Growth and Benefit

*I*f you're able to let go enough, to surrender enough, you have the opportunity to change the way you look at your life and proceed with an expanded consciousness that is more attuned to your Higher Power. You also have the opportunity to emerge into the happiness that keeps on shining like the sun. Wouldn't it be nice to be, not at the effect of things, but closer to the cause? Remember, being attached to a vision of things happening a certain way is setting yourself up for unhappiness. Happiness is staying attuned to your spiritual center, regardless of what happens. And it can be something more. By developing the virtue soon to be disclosed in this chapter, you can experience further happiness by discovering the good spiritual fortune inherent in whatever happens.

If you're practicing surrender, you are practicing detaching yourself from what is happening and from the results. You're rising above judgments and narrow agendas sourced in ego. If your main commitment is shifting your attitude to thinking, "I accept that whatever is happening is best for my spiritual growth, and I surrender lovingly to the flow of my life," your perspective is shifting to being spiritually informed. If, for instance, your airline flight is canceled, rather than being upset and ranting about the increasing inefficiency of the airlines, you may think, "This was for my ultimate good, and if I remain open, I may be shown why." See how life can shift from drudgery into adventure? Another example: If you don't get a job that you thought was really great, you may think, "This was for my ultimate good, and I can discover a better opportunity while strengthening virtues such as adjusting, patience, and surrender."

Despite concentrated contemplation, you may not discover why things happen the way they do. That's because, for most of us, a veil separates us from true spiritual insight into actual cause and effect. Most of us can just lean into an appreciation of the way that life works out. This is the great challenge for developing faith and an appreciation of the goodness of God. Yet, we each possess the faculty to develop spiritually and learn to know, and ultimately, to *really know*. Therefore, if you're cultivating detachment and inculcating the virtues, you're developing the ability to successfully negotiate challenges of your life. You're not growing in self-righteous bitterness but flowering as a spiritual being. You are advancing in this school of life, preparing yourself for your next *higher* level and utilizing *discrimination*.

*Discrimination* is simply the ability to utilize whatever happens for your spiritual growth. It is the ability to see beyond appearances and perceive whether something is beneficial or harmful to your spiritual progress. When you become adept at discrimination, you can perceive how something that is outwardly not to your liking may actually help you progress spiritually and how something outwardly inviting may impede your progress. It is not easy, because we are very attached to things and to things happening a certain way.

By practicing discrimination and the other virtues of Spirituality without Judgment, you can develop spiritual maturity. This is a challenge that you can meet successfully. As you practice putting your spirituality first, your outlook—that is, your way of looking out at yourself in the world—becomes clearer, so that, by practicing discrimination, you facilitate your spiritual progress. As part of this, your abiding genuine happiness also emerges. Are you ready to practice?

## ❖ Exercise ❖

Look at something you don't like as being for your spiritual growth and benefit. Choose something in your life that's not happening the way you want it to. It could be a promotion that's not coming through, the loss of an account, the failure of someone to live up to a commitment, or the failure of someone to be or respond to you a certain way. Choose whatever is now rankling you the most.

Visualize the person, the events, the whole situation and your place in them. Allow yourself to feel whatever feelings come up, such as disappointment, loss, frustration, or anger. While seeing yourself in the situation, also realize that, at the same time, you're simultaneously outside the situation.

Look at yourself with love and compassion for what you're going through. If, for instance, you didn't get a job that you really wanted, affirm with utter conviction, "This is for my spiritual benefit." Now, be a mystical sleuth and, from your detached vantage point, look behind the scenes to see why you didn't get the job. You'll probably see a whole combination of possible factors: the job is, after all, going to be temporary; you would have gotten into a situation that is going to turn ugly; there's a better job opening up down the road; you have work to perform elsewhere; and so on. Just uncover all the possible reasons why what you wanted didn't happen. It may just be that you have other growth to go through first and this is not the proper time.

You may now feel that you know why you didn't get the job. You may not. Have faith that, if you are to know, it will be revealed to you at the right time. Ponder the following three questions.

1. What spiritual lessons can this experience provide?

2. Which spiritual virtues does this experience give me the opportunity to inculcate?

3. How does this experience provide for my spiritual growth and benefit?

By looking at the situation objectively, you're developing discrimination. You're not getting stuck in what happened, but accepting it. You're continuing on your spiritual path, committed and not looking back, because you've experienced your feelings of disappointment, worked through them, and opened up to knowing why something that you initially did not like may be for your spiritual growth and benefit. As you practice discrimination in responding to events in your life and making choices, you'll also start practicing discrimination in regard to people.

Practicing discrimination with people can be difficult. But it's particularly helpful if you've developed your true vision of self-realization for yourself. To further your emerging spirituality, you may decide to keep the company of spiritually minded people. The company that you keep exerts a tremendous influence on you. For example, solid, grounded, and sober honor students have died of alcohol poisoning by allowing peer pressure to undermine their integrity and discrimination. Friends and fellow travelers may exert subtle yet pervasive and seemingly good-intentioned pressure that their way is the right way, that they know best. But do they know what is best for you? They may have logged decades of service and deservedly occupy unimpeachable positions of authority in charitable organizations, but are they beyond egotism? Do they come from a place of pure love, of fully realized soul?

Unless you really know that they do, you may need to remain alert in this good, spiritual company as well as in your old, worldly, down-pulling company, and listen to that still, sure voice within. When you're in conflict, when you're not sure what is the right way, you may serve yourself best not by following the self-anointed leaders or the privileged herd but by concentrating within yourself and rekindling your commitment to your spiritual growth, no matter what. Then feel from what direction your heart is gladdened, your love is revived, your path is cleared. This is discrimination.

# NINE

# *Forgiveness*

# *and Love*

# Forgive Someone
# Who Has Hurt You

Remember the old saying "To err is human; to forgive divine"? People are prone to error. If we were perfect, we wouldn't be here—we'd be with the Creator.

In spirituality, we aim to achieve perfection step by step, thought by thought, action by action. Most people mean well, and if, when they hurt you, they don't mean well, they are probably acting out of a former unresolved hurt. That hurt came from your relationship with them, from other relationships like it, from a family relationship, or from some combination of all of these. Thus, in relationships where hurt has been wrapped around everything, remember the frailty of your fellow struggling humans and develop compassion. In relationships where there has been unpleasantness, even ugliness, there's no doubt been lack of forgiveness. And compassion is necessary for forgiveness.

## ❖ Activity ❖

Forgive someone who has hurt you. Think of all the people with whom you're unhappy. Choose one person toward whom you feel residual anger about how that person acted toward you or how you perceive that the person acted toward you. That person should also be someone to whom you'd like to be closer. When you've resolved what stands between you both, you'll feel lighter and more in the present, better able to pursue your spiritual work.

Even though forgiveness is the antidote to anger, moving from anger to forgiveness may not be as easy as moving from point A to point B. You may need to get as clear as possible on the incidents that prompted the anger, and then feel and work through the shock, hurt, outrage, and resentment before entering the stages of exploration, information gathering, discovery, understanding, and compassion. Thus, if you're feeling a certain residual anger toward the person, it's probably best to first process the anger before you endeavor to develop compassion and forgive the person. Particularly, if it's clear that you need to meet with the person to practice forgiveness, you may wish to process your anger in privacy because the person may find it difficult to feel your forgiveness if you're venting rage.

## ❖ Optional Process ❖

Develop and practice processes that enable you to fully express your anger toward the person whom you wish to forgive. Do whatever will give you a complete release. Reenact the incidents that led to your hurt. Then, using your creative imagination, at a time when you're assured that you won't be heard, visualize the person in a chair in the privacy of your home, and let it all hang out. Lecture, yell, tell how much the person hurt you, howl, kick, slap, or spit. Oh, doesn't it feel good? Express every bit of anger and outrage, feel a lot of energy move, and feel your breath moving freely through your body.

## ❖ Continuing Process ❖

You may wish to write a letter to the person who hurt you, getting it all down on paper, without ever sending it. You may wish to write first before visualizing the person, to organize your thoughts and feelings and experience the satisfaction of articulating perfectly how you were hurt. You may wish to get very physical and use a plastic bat to beat up your bed. Or, you may feel complete doing the entire process through visualization, telling the person off and striking them without lifting a finger. The point is, do whatever it takes to experience and process your anger in private so that you are ready to move to a higher level that will defuse the judgments that led to that anger.

You may now be far better able to develop compassion. Not just intellectual compassion but also heart-felt compassion. Since it's difficult to develop compassion in the abstract, when you've been feeling everything but, you'll want to learn about the injuring party's situation to gain understanding. Thus, in addition to thinking objectively about the person and exploring the truth behind the hurtful incidents, it may be a good idea to talk to mutual friends to gather information to better understand the person and situation. However, probably nothing can produce better results than *communicating directly with the person in a nonpressured, nonjudgmental way*. Meet with the person in a private, nonconfrontational manner, and explain that you wish to understand the hurtful behavior. Ask that person to explain their experience of the situation. Do your best to allow the other person to open up and explain the behavior as they view it and to share the truth of their experience.

By discovering the truth of the other party's experience, you can gain understanding and at least some appreciation of why that person acted as they did or failed to act as you deemed appropriate. You can feel what the person was struggling with when they acted that way. From this higher vantage point, the anger and hurt around that person will get decharged because the judgments that gave rise to the anger can get tossed out. By understanding that person, compassion can come, and even though you may not ultimately agree with what the person did, from that genuine feeling of compassion, forgiveness can come and heal that relationship.

With forgiveness comes healing or wholing—being made whole—for love can now re-circulate. You'll also be better able to explain your experience by relating it in statements that begin, "I felt such-and-such when you. . . . " Thus, you can actually give the other person the gift of knowing why you were mad, withdrawn, breaking agreements, backbiting, and so on. Through such honest, nonjudgmental communication can come the gift of love.

*Forgiving others* is a foundational practice of spirituality, for it removes judgments that have hardened into debts that must be paid. Use whatever process works best for you—quiet contemplation or active communication. But, by *forgiving others*, you are severing the ropes that bind you and inviting the winds of love to uplift you. Thus, you are pleasing your Higher Power and rising in that consciousness.

You're also inviting the conditions under which others may forgive you. Ultimately, don't we want forgiveness for ourselves?

Don't we prefer forgiveness to having to pay for our wrongs with justice? It's easy to want justice from the party who has supposedly wronged us, but how willing are we to pay for our own wrongs with the wronged party's idea of justice?

The idea of forgiveness is that you are forgoing the seeking of justice. Seeking justice is really a term for seeking retribution. It may be active, such as hurting the other person physically, verbally, or with judgments; or passive, such as withholding feelings and communication. How can the score ever be settled by seeking justice? What you deem fair, the other party will feel is an infringment and will then seek payment in kind or, usually, worse. By seeking justice, you can start an unending downward spiral of tit for tat, judgment for judgment, blow for blow, an obsessive maelstrom that sucks in all your energy and goodness.

You may eventually derive some satisfaction by seeking justice, legally or on your own, but it is far better to seek mercy and forgiveness. That is what is given in the Court of the Lord.

By forgiving others, you are dealing in the currency of the Court of Love. That's far superior to the mental satisfaction of justice. We only have limited time here in these bodies. Before they are relinquished, do you wish to be consumed with lust for revenge and justice, or do you wish to resolve your differences, forgive others, and usher in love?

# Get Ready
# to Leave
# in Three Days

Pretend that you hear a sweet, loving voice from inside you call your name. The voice calls you again and says, "In three days, I will take you. In three days, your sojourn here will end."

For now, really believe this. What do you feel? After experiencing the myriad feelings this brings up, reflect on how you've spent your life. What have you accomplished? What haven't you accomplished? How have you treated others? Are there situations or relationships in which you wish you'd behaved differently?

If you faithfully follow this exercise and the following activity, it can be extremely powerful for you. Feel free to repeat the exercise and your responses to the above and following questions. After you've reviewed these questions, go about your life with the secret notion that you have three remaining days in which to live. Let yourself do whatever you need to do to feel that you're completing your stay here. What can you give yourself that will let you feel complete? For instance, you may wish to take one last look at beloved photographs, treat yourself to strawberries and whipped cream, or watch a sunset from your favorite vantage point.

Also, remembering your responses to these questions, go about your business, yet make it your business to complete unfinished business. Not only your business in the world but also people business. Hopefully, pretty soon, the fact that your estate is not in order should pale beside the fact that, in *three days*, you're going to leave all those people in your life. Now, two days. Okay, one day. Don't tell anyone. Keep it a secret. How do you wish to act toward the people in your life? All of a sudden, the things that stand between you may become insignificant. How much more interested are you in seeking forgiveness and forgiving others? When you know that you're going to leave soon, very soon, forgiveness becomes paramount. And if forgiveness is not an issue, then what communication is absolutely crucial?

That you love them. Show it or speak it. What matters, really? The love between you. If love is the essence of spirituality, then *loving others* is its expression toward your fellow souls struggling in this world. *Loving others* is the natural flow, the crucial expression of your inner condition, the essence of your soul.

## ❖ Activity ❖

Treat everyone lovingly for the next three days. As you get ready to leave this earthly existence, as you go about your business, treat everyone lovingly. No matter whom you come in contact with, however seemingly insignificant or out-of-line they are, treat them lovingly. Look at each person with whom you interact as a particle of God, containing a flame of God's love. Recalling your good work with the virtue agenting, look at yourself as God's representative, called on to give God's Love.

While driving, give other drivers the chance to pull out into traffic. While at your job, work as though your main mission, as entrusted to you by God, is not to make money but to accomplish your work goals *in harmony, with love prevailing*. While at the market, rather than beat your fellow shoppers to the strawberries, give them a smile, and give your cashier some kind words. Plan special get-togethers with your friends and family, and let them experience your acceptance of them and your gratitude for their being fellow travelers on this journey and your teachers as provided by God. Treat them all lovingly.

This is your challenge and opportunity. It's one thing to act lovingly toward a friendly salesperson to whom you're giving a big sale. It's another to act lovingly toward a family member with whom you have a twisted history of hurts. Remember, uppermost, that love is a function of forgiveness and communication.

If something stands between you and another, see the divinity and human frailty of that person, practice forgiveness, and communicate to work out what stands between you. In so doing, you are replacing the debilitating webs of hurt with the revitalizing bonds of love.

By loving others, we get to pass on lessons in this schoolhouse of life. Loving others is the virtue that is so hard to embody yet crucial for advancing in our spirituality. In loving others, we elevate others as well as ourselves and grow closer to our Higher Power. We experience consciously that mysterious, mystical, joyful essence that is life and God. We rise and transcend our false barriers to enjoy the Oneness that, even if long-forgotten, we still crave deep down in our cores.

When your three days are up, you may find yourself still alive. Be grateful for everything that you've been given and for the expanded consciousness of how you can better live out your remaining days in this life. For you are leaving. It is a matter of days. It may very well be several thousand or merely several. But one day you will leave. Let's hope that you work toward that day, making your barriers fall, while in that freed space, you exercise the spiritual imperative of loving others.

# The Next Time You Feel Unloved, Enter Your Temple

The next time you feel unloved, find a quiet time when you can be undisturbed and unaware of others. Let yourself feel that unlove, that hurt, that pain. Now, open your heart. Put your consciousness in your heart and open it to God. Feel the tenderness and softness of your heart, and give that pain to God. Think of your body as a temple, the place where you go to worship, and your heart as the living center of that temple. Your living, beating heart is the place where you go to triumph and rise above all the trials and tribulations that you have had to suffer. Finally, they matter only insofar as they can bring you closer to the source of all-abiding Love.

Feel your heart and any pain of being unloved. However you visualize God, send forth love to God. With body, mind, and soul, marshal every bit of love and will that you have to generate and send love. Make *loving God* your religion.

The word "religion" comes from the Latin *religare* and means "to bind." We fulfill the promise of true religion when we bind back our consciousness, our souls, to God. This is the true journey of religion. From our limited, individuated consciousnesses of pain and pleasure, we begin to transcend these narrow confines of sensation and awaken to the unlimited consciousness of our Higher Power. Though we may not personally know someone who has completed the long, arduous, wondrous journey or even someone who has made much progress, this immersing and realizing is a journey that is available to each soul. Though the details of the experiences along the way may be unique to each soul, the common thread is a growing love of God. *Love means to lose your identity and to become one with the Beloved*. Thus, we begin to achieve true spirituality when we begin to lose ourselves in *loving God*.

Each day, one opportunity to practice this virtue follows another. By concentrating on loving God rather than on getting the fruits of our worship, we progress. If loving God feels too abstract or distant, practice loving Jesus Christ or a Saint to whom you are specially connected. Whomever you focus on, know with unshakable assurance that your Beloved is your *true friend, your loving friend*. That Power loves you more than you can conceive.

Also, please remember that the joy, the bliss that passes understanding, is in the loving, not in the receiving. Shun every expectation that rears its head and would lure you away from the present and your practice. Don't get caught in the trap of expecting a divine visitation for all the good things you've done and the efforts you've made. Be the lover who wants only to give time and attention, expecting nothing. Be the lover, thinking nothing of yourself as you open yourself to loving God. Be the lover whose heart keeps growing and expanding, to be subsumed by God, so that anything is possible. And be the lover who is so fully absorbed in your love that you would run to your Beloved lightly over the heads of crocodiles, unaware of any danger.

When you feel unloved, it's usually because you want and expect love from a particular source outside yourself and you are not getting it. Perhaps your partner did not kiss you upon coming home. Perhaps your partner hasn't said, "I love you" for a week or a month or several years. Somehow, your expectations are going unfulfilled and your needs are left wanting. But here, you are concentrating on receiving, while love only knows how to give. If your emphasis is on receiving, on getting what you want, you're strengthening your ego. Love is giving, and losing your ego. Love is no quid pro quo, where each tit demands a tat. Love is losing yourself in the Beloved. Rather than concentrating on the getting, concentrate on the giving, on the absorption in your Beloved.

## ❖ Exercise ❖

Find a quiet time, sit comfortably, close your eyes, enter your temple, and practice devotion. Know that you can create the most beautiful flowers and fragrances for your Beloved. With full intention and attention, contemplate on your Higher Power or a particular Saint. With each remembrance, let a beautiful rose flower from your thought and rest on your lap. Your love is so intent, so powerful, that the roses are devoid of thorns. Your love is so expressive that every gradation of emotion forms a rose of a different hue. In your mind's eye, once you have a full bouquet, offer that bouquet to your Beloved, with all your love.

## ❖ Activity ❖

If there's a person in your life with whom you're not satisfied, why not give that person a bouquet of flowers or do something that they will really appreciate? For a time, transcend judgments that have hardened from unmet expectations. Do something simple, like preparing a favorite meal, giving flowers, or accompanying that person in an activity that they really appreciate. Do something with the aim of bringing joy to that person. Practice the spiritual quality of agenting, discreetly extending your connection to God to them.

By acting selflessly and lovingly, you're also practicing the all-abiding spiritual quality of loving God. We are all of God and we are all connected. By practicing love in action with those who've been placed close to you in your life, you are growing in your love of God. And the more your love grows, the more you are being readied for that never-ending symphony of love of being subsumed by God and raised in that Power.

# Onward

Balance. Concentration. Grace. Knowledge. Truth. Peace. Love. Bliss.

These are some of the names we use to describe the outcome of a spiritual life. But those words, the names of states of consciousness, are just words. They comprise an outer game of trying to convey and understand the inner transformation. That inner transformation, that winning of grace and higher consciousness, is the result of the inner and outer practice of sounding the notes of love.

Playing the notes of the spiritual scale . . . concentrating, flowing, recentering the attention, heeding the inner calls . . . lets spaces open up where the ego falls back and allows the spiritual senses to awaken and be tuned. We are but the instruments, discordant from improper use, yet capable of the finest music. Within each of us is the celestial melody, streaming through us, capable of being heard and heard more clearly the better we are turned within and tuned.

Even after we devote ourselves to a growing spiritual life, we still hear and play the coarse outer strains of sensuality and materialism. They're loud, compelling in their grossness, habitual, and familiar. And everyone else seems to be rushing heedlessly after these worldly strains, neither noticing nor caring that they muffle our subtle spiritual notes. Yet, for those who keep practicing the virtues and listening to their finer inner music, the worldly songs turn into strident noise. And when we become truly weary of those unsatisfying songs, then we decide, we just want the soft spiritual music and will continually seek something better.

We dedicate ourselves to our search for truth and to awakening our Self. We adopt practices and routines and disciplines and do our best to purify our character. We work. We await results. We confront nothingness. We give up. We laugh at ourselves, try again, fail, and then give up again. We get pulled away and work harder to come back to our true work. We sweat tears, swearing that this is impossible. We ask, whatever happened to inner guidance, let alone results? Then, when we're bone weary, when we've stayed true and given our all and accepted nothing, from far off, we again catch snatches of a finer music, a melody that so entrances and awakens long-forgotten memories that we wish to follow wherever it may lead.

We explore anew. We rededicate ourselves to the work. We discover new strengths and virtues. We grow in maturity and patience. We understand better that the work is nothing but cleaning the instrument for the receiving of grace. We notice that as we attend to the spiritual work, the worldly work proceeds smoothly because it is performed from a spiritual vantage. It's as if the boundaries between the inner and worldly music are disappearing, and we come to realize that it's all of a piece and all of a purpose. We simultaneously attend to the worldly and to the inner work, moment by moment, breath by breath.

Sometimes, our shortcomings leave us breathless. We seem worse than ever before. We may seem to be backsliding, slipping out of rhythm and out of sync. But think of it as slowly turning up a dimmer switch in a dark room that hasn't been cleaned for years. As the light grows, the mess and dirt and disorder become apparent and glare back. The growing light helps us see things and remember things that are now within our vision. The growing light, too, helps strengthen our sight for still stronger light and for still subtler things. That is good. Continue the work. Do the everyday things to inculcate spiritual qualities. Accept the more challenging challenges.

All spiritual practices are good. We may not seem to be improving, but those close to us may observe the growth and appreciate the sweeter sounds and silences of our soul. Our inability to recognize our improvement is fine because it may mean that we are truly growing in humility. And in humble gratitude, we may realize that we prefer to forgive, to render service, to be truthful and nonviolent and open to quiet joy. Our heart is being healed. Our mind is being cleansed. Life-giving grace is reaching our soul.

Keep practicing; keep playing the melody, for this is the prelude to an awakened inner life of true celestial music and light. For when we can take the brilliance, we can come to know that God is the Music, is the Instrument, is the Player. Ultimately, when we surrender to and become that never-ending symphony, we can win a life that takes us Home—right to the heart of the Love of God. And that is the source of all Bliss.

# ACKNOWLEDGMENTS

I gratefully thank and acknowledge:

My agent, Frances Kuffel, for recognizing the value of this project and finding its best home.

Brian Hines, Diane Frary, Vicki Broach, Letitia Wiley, Matthew Seal, Kaylene Tobin, Jane Clarke, and Jana Denegri for reading a draft of the manuscript and giving me helpful feedback.

My editor, Ken Winston Caine, for stepping in at the 10th hour and doing a splendid job.

Cynthe Brush, Bill Grey, Jane Pritchard, Carmen Mobieus, Richard Metz, James Arena, and my mother for their love and support during the process.

Brian Hines and Matthew Seal for being superlative sounding boards and sharing their discernment.

Diane Frary for her love and support, her inspiring advocacy, and her knowledge.

H, SJ, BJS, BM, JS, and BJ for being there and for their true inspiration.

# GUIDE TO THE
# 33 SPIRITUAL VIRTUES

# ABOUT THE AUTHOR

Michael Goddart began at age 10 to consciously seek and practice his spiritual path. For 30 years, he has studied the teachings of Saints and practiced the disciplines given by living Masters. His spiritual odyssey and work as a consultant have taken him to more than 40 countries, allowing him to sojourn and study with realized Saints. He has a masters degree of fine arts from the Writers Workshop at Bowling Green State University in Ohio, and his articles have appeared in international spiritual journals. He is the author of *Spiritual Revolution: A Seeker's Guide; 52 Powerful Principles for Your Mind and Soul*.

The author would like to hear from you regarding ways you've found to develop particular spiritual virtues and strengths. Please send your stories to:

mgoddart@goddart.com

or

Michael Goddart

c/o Clear Path

P. O. Box 2333

Santa Rosa, CA 95405-0333

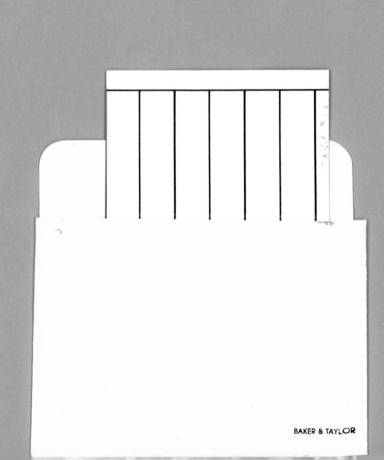